Discover THE REAL YOU

Release Past Hurts, Negative Habits, and Hang-Ups

Farraday Williams

Copyright © 2021 by Farraday Williams

Discover the Real You: Release Past Hurts, Negative Habits, and Hang-ups

All rights reserved. No part of this publication may be reproduced, distributed, or transmitted in any form or by any means, including photocopying, recording, or other electronic or mechanical methods, without the prior written permission of the publisher, Bible Media Press Publishing, except in the case of brief quotations embodied in critical reviews and certain other noncommercial uses permitted by copyright law. Contact Bible Media Press Publishing at biblemediapresspublishing@gmail.com.

Although the author and publisher have made every effort to ensure that the information in this book was correct at press time, the author and publisher do not assume and hereby disclaim any liability to any party for any loss, damage, or disruption caused by errors or omissions, whether such errors or omissions result from negligence, accident, or any other cause.

Adherence to all applicable laws and regulations, including international, federal, state, and local governing professional licensing, business practices, advertising, and all other aspects of doing business in the US, Canada, or any other jurisdiction, is the sole responsibility of the reader and consumer.

Neither the author nor the publisher assumes any responsibility or liability whatsoever on behalf of the consumer or reader of this material. Any perceived slight of any individual or organization is purely unintentional.

Scripture quotations marked NIV are taken from the Holy Bible, New International Version®, copyright ©1973, 1978, 1984, 2011 by Biblica, Inc.™ Used by permission of Zondervan. The NIV and New International Version are trademarks registered in the United States Patent and Trademark Office by Biblica, Inc.™

Scripture quotations marked CSB have been taken from the Christian Standard Bible®, copyright © 2017 by Holman Bible Publishers. Used by permission. Christian Standard Bible® and CSB® are federally registered trademarks of Holman Bible Publishers.

Scripture quotations marked NLT are taken from the Holy Bible, New Living Translation, copyright © 1996, 2004, 2015 by Tyndale House Foundation. Used by permission of Tyndale House Publishers, Carol Stream, Illinois 60188. All rights reserved.

Scripture marked KJV are taken from the King James Version®, copyright © 1982 by Thomas Nelson. Used by permission. All rights reserved.

Scripture quotations marked ESV are taken from The Holy Bible, English Standard Version®, copyright © 2001 by Crossway Bibles, a publishing ministry of Good News Publishers. Used by permission. All rights reserved

ISBN: 978-1-956396-02-7 (Paperback)
ISBN: 978-1-956396-00-3 (Hardback)
ISBN: 978-1-956396-01-0 (eBook)

Library of Congress Number: 2021920459

For Worldwide Distribution for God's Kingdom. Printed in the U.S.A.

Dedication

Elizabeth Williams, November 30, 1931–January 15, 2020

First, I would like to dedicate this book to Father God, the Holy Spirit, and my dear and precious Lord and Savior, Jesus Christ.

Second, I dedicate this book in memory of one of God's faithful servants, my Queen of a Mom.

As my mom always said,

> *"Son, you can do or be anybody you want to be in life if you keep putting God first, as you strive forward giving Him 100 percent and all that you got."*

A Queen of a Mom

by Farraday Williams

Every day I think of you, Mom, in such a special way:
How we would get up and plan nice things to do together,
each and every day,
things like going to the beauty shop to get you A Queen
Bee pedicure and manicure,
Always having lots of fun as the people would say, "How
can I help you, dear?"
But now I must wake up each day, Mom, and plan them
all alone,
But I'll still reminisce on the wonderful times we have
shared together while singing different gospel songs.
One thing I can truly say, and I mean it from my heart,
I always knew you were one of a kind, a Queen of a
Mom, from the very start.
You cared so much for others, and you joked and had lots
of fun.
You would never leave anybody out until your work was
done.
So now, Mom, I wrote this to you in the form of a poem,
and the biggest message that I want you to know is that
you were
one Queen of a Mom.

Acknowledgments

Several people and organizations have been a tremendous influence throughout my life and have been an incredible blessing to me writing this book. So, I would like to thank you all.

To all of the ministries and speakers on the Trinity Broadcast Networks and all of the people who spread the good news about Jesus Christ, thank you so very much. Your examples have inspired me to keep reaching toward the sky and use my talents and spiritual gifts to build God's Kingdom.

Paul, Jan, Matt, and Laurie Crouch, thank you and your dear dad and mom for your phenomenal ministry, Trinity Broadcasting Network. My dad and I have been following and supporting this ministry for years, and you guys were part of the catalyst in bringing me to the Lord through my dear dad's prayers and support. Thanks for touching so many lives through your ministry.

Joel Osteen, thanks for your ministry and inspirational books. I have them all. It's impossible to watch you, listen to you, or read one of your uplifting books and not be super excited and positive about life and God. They all have truly inspired me to reach my full potential and learn how to make "everyday a Friday!"

Bishop T.D. Jakes, I have practically all your books, and your ministry has been very beneficial in inspiring me to keep soaring to reach my full potential in God. Your encouragement has been a very pivotal part of my faith growing and my striving toward my destiny.

Joyce Meyer, Wow! You are, and have been, a phenomenal inspiration to me in so many ways. Your ministry and resources have given me the courage and unshakable trust and faith to write this book while learning how to fight the battlefield of the mind.

Charles F. Stanley, I want to thank your In Touch Ministry and you for creating your Life Principle Bibles. I have bought over one hundred of them as gifts to many others because it is one of the greatest informative ministering tools available. It was very instrumental in preparing me to write this book and in helping me to develop an intimate relationship with Christ.

Tyler Perry, thanks for being such a great example of who you can be if you hold onto your dreams, learn that "Higher is waiting," and believe in the grace of God. Your accomplishments, plays, books, and movies have always encouraged me to do more and to keep searching for my purpose in life.

My Beloved dad, Clarence L. Williams Sr. (Do boy) Thanks for your faithful prayers, support, and for giving me my first Gold Leaf Bible. I will always love you.

My Beloved Wife, Shirley B. Williams, and my Awesome Kids, Marquice and Farrah Williams -thanks for traveling with me through many trials and journeys in my life. You three have been my encouragement and inspiration for sharing my tremendous adventures through many adversities and hardships. I love you dearly.

Mr. R.A. Apffel, my attorney and adopted dad, you have been a strong endurable boat beneath my sails. You have always believed in me and supplied me with the necessary fuel, encouragement, and advice to endure so many trials in my life. Thanks for inspiring me to write my life story to bless many others and leave a legacy for our future generations. Much love to you and yours.

My God Parents: (Jessie W. and Mary Ida Lyons) -thanks for inspiring me to always keep striving and following my dreams.

My Dear and Precious, God Sister: Dr. Jeri Lyons- Thanks for always being such a positive inspiration and influence in my life, and for always reminding me that "I Can Do It!"

Patricia Farris, thanks for being so sympathetic to me during some of my darkest moments when I had to deal with the house in Galveston, Texas, and my Queen of a Mom's illness. I could not have made it through those situations and adversities without your help, encouragement, and support.

Rosalind G. Stephens, no words can express the love and gratitude for you walking with me through each phase of my life's journey. I love you dearly.

Pastor Harry and Corliss Allen, thank you both for your support. Corliss, you are one incredible and very powerful praying cousin who walked with me daily as we experienced God's miraculous power to bring me through some of the most devastating times in my life. Thank you dearly.

Clarence L. Williams Jr. my oldest brother, and your precious wife, Anita, I love you both from the bottom of my heart. Thanks, my dear brother, for being there for me through it all.

James Kirk Williams, my youngest brother, , and awesome wife, Rhonda thank you for your help and support throughout my life. Much love to you and yours.

Latoya and Clarence III, my dear niece and nephew, thanks for supporting me through my mom's illness and encouraging me to write this book. I love you both.

To Mr. Thomas Kinkade and his family, gallery owners, staff members, wonderful collectors, and master highlighters, thanks for being a valuable part of my story and life. I love and miss every one of you. Thanks for the wonderful experiences.

Mr. Charles H. White, thanks for being my art mentor and encouraging me to keep striving toward fulfilling my life's destiny. I will always be grateful to you.

Mr. Eric Rhoads, thanks for the motivation and outstanding example of following your dreams and becoming a successful entrepreneur.

Chuck Hayward, thank you for being sensitive to the Holy Spirit and inviting me to lunch to tell me your thoughts about bringing my Queen of a Mom back to live with me in California. It was one of the best decisions that I made in life.

Thanks also to:
- Family Community Church, Pastor Chester McGensy, and lovely wife Janetta, and members.
- Celebrate Recovery Groups

- Madera Men of Integrity Group
- All of Madera local churches
- Madera Rescue Mission staff and guests
- My mighty prayer warrior team
- CMS Welding and Machining and its employees, Georgia Pacific /Color Box and employees, Ardagh Group and employees

Additionally, I have so many people to thank for helping me in writing this book that the list would become another book within itself. Still, I would like to at least thank the following people and organizations for being an essential part of my life and helping to make this book possible.

Katie Chambers of Beacon Point LLC, thank you so much for making my first of many books come to life. Your expertise has added so much more superb value to my book. Thanks for being my tremendous beacon of light. I would eagerly recommend any upcoming or experienced authors to use your fantastic editing services. Thanks again.

Chandler Bolt and Self-Publishing School, thanks to you and your wonderful team for providing me with the necessary tools to create my book.

Joris Van Leeuwen and Danijela Mijailovic of Cutting-Edge Studio, thanks for your wonderful services and cover design. You guys are awesome.

I would like to thank everyone with whom I have crossed paths during my phenomenal journeys and adventures. I want to thank you all for being a part of my life.

Finally, I would like to acknowledge every reader of this book and thank you in advance for reading it. I would like to encourage you to keep striving toward reaching your full potential in God as you discover the real you in Christ.

A Special Gift

Thank you for reading

Discover the Real You, Release Past Hurts, Negative Habits, and Hang-Ups.

Receive a free Interlude:
"Your Turn Releasing Past Hurts, Negative Habits, and Hang-Ups" at farradaywilliamsauthor.com.

Additional Information

How to use and get the most out of this book:

For those of you who want to deal specifically with releasing past hurts, negative habits, and hang-ups, in the Interlude, you will find some practical methods and steps to help you head toward a life of freedom, fulfillment, and victory as you learn how to reach your full potential in Christ and begin to discover the real you.

Then in parts one and two, I encourage you to explore the things to think about, scriptures to study, and the questions to answer to help you grow in your relationship with Christ.

I pray that the interactive questions will help you relate to my testimony and life experiences deeper and help you learn how to respond to any problems correctly.

Contents

Introduction 13

Part 1:
 The Shoot Level—Self-Growth Stage 15
 An Arrow to the Head 15
 Lessons in Football 18
 The Discovery on the Trail 21
 The Power of Love 25
 The Power of Prayer 28
 Love Never Fails 31

Part 2:
 The Sapling Level— (Developing Stage) 37
 Prayer Changes Things 37
 The Road to Transformation 42
 My Wilderness Journey 45
 My Faith Journey 47
 Walking by Faith Part 1 53
 Walking by Faith Part 2 59
 Having Faith in God's Promises   64

Interlude:
 Your Turn 71
 Releasing Past Hurts 71
 Releasing the Negative Habits and Hang-Ups 76

xi

Part 3:
- The Blooming Level (Maturing Stage)........................79
- God's Restoration Process 79
- Traveling Ambassadors of Light Adventures 82
- Family Meetings 86
- Then Cometh Pride..88
- Courage through Adversity and Hardships 88
- The Golden Journey 92
- The Golden Walk 99
- The Golden Crown 101

Conclusion:
- Your Turn to Discover the..109
- Real You in Christ... 109
- Salvation Is Key to Obtaining Your Helper 110
- New Creation in Christ 110
- Renewing of the Mind 111
- The Value of God's Word 112
- We Must Learn to Walk By Faith................................ 113
- We Are in a Spiritual War 114
- Keep Feeding Your Spiritual Baby............................115
- I Will Fear No Evil 116
- I Will Never Forsake You or Leave You....................117

Let's Connect 119

How Can You Help? 121

About the author 123

Introduction

This is your pathway to fulfilling the destiny that awaits you as you learn how to discover the real you and release past hurts, negative habits, and hang-ups in your life.

Are you tired of responding the wrong way to peer pressure, insecurity, self-pride, anger, and unforgiveness?

Well, buckle up, and come along with me on these breathtaking journeys as I give you some key principles and skills that will help you unpack and process through your struggles and springboard forward into reaching your full potential in God.

First, I want you to come along with me on my life's journeys, which I will depict in three stages of a tree:

- the shoot level (self-growth stage)
- the sapling level (developing stage)
- the blooming level (maturing stage)

Even after this last stage, realize you are still a work in process. You will be continually learning during your entire life journey.

Part 1 introduces the shoot level (self-growth stage) of my life and represents the beginning stage when I was still very young, naive, and quite foolish. I had no real sense of direction other than what I was told by my parents or others who influenced my behavior. As a result, I was mostly focusing on myself during this stage of my life.

In these first few stories, I give you a snapshot of my life experiences, mainly dealing with peer pressure and insecurity, anger, unforgiveness, self-pride, and fear.

During this beginning stage of my life, I had to learn how to navigate through life in such a way as to try to alleviate as many hurts, negative habits, and hang-ups as possible.

Part 2 is about the sapling level (developing stage), the time in my life when I went through many transitions. I had to go on an extraordinary journey to find my identity in Christ while learning how to deal with the negative emotions that hindered me and caused many character defects to resurface in my life. God took me through many roads of transformation, allowing me to experience many faith journeys and faith walks with Him. During this time, I was beginning to know God and believe He could restore my life to a life of wholeness.

You, too, can find a life of freedom and wholeness and begin to strive forward toward reaching your full potential in God as you learn how to discover the real you and release past hurts, negative habits, and hang-ups.

Part 3 addresses the blooming level (maturing stage), which represents a time in my life when God's restoration process with my family had begun, and I was growing and maturing in my life as I traveled across the country as one of God's traveling ambassadors of light and master highlighters for Mr. Thomas Kinkade. I also created family meetings for my family to help them grow in their faith and life. Through this time, I went through extraordinary adventures that led me to discover the real me and develop an intimate relationship with Jesus Christ through His precious Holy Spirit.

So, my dear readers, the time has come for you to read and embrace some of these valuable insights in this book and allow God, through His Holy Spirit, to help launch you into fulfilling your life's dreams as you reach your full potential and discover the real you in Christ.

Part 1:
The Shoot Level—Self-Growth Stage

It all started in Galveston, Texas, where I was born to Clarence and Elizabeth Williams. According to my dear mom, my parents were doing fine until my father entered the service and came back with all kinds of bad attitudes and bad habits. This led to their separation. So, my mom, older brother, and I went to Fort Worth to live with my mother's sister and started our lives again. My mom had few skills but an incredible belief and faith in God. She felt that no matter what she decided to do, she could always ask for the good Lord's help, and he would give her some direction. She had always taught my brother and me to pray to the Lord at bedtime and thank Him in the morning for giving us another day.

Well, here my dear brother and I were living in a new and strange land for us. I was a little young at the time, so it did not matter much to me where I was if I was somewhere close to my mama.

An Arrow to the Head

The first time I experienced peer pressure was playing war with my brother and friends in an old, abandoned house. We gathered our weapons. My younger friends were positioned on the top of the house, and my brother and his older friends were positioned inside the house.

Since it was an abandoned house, there were numerous holes in the rooftop, allowing us to see the other team inside walking through the rooms. We all had, what we called at the time, tomahawks, which were giant stalks with roots pulled up from the ground with large clogs of dirt attached to them. My brother's team had bows, and they used long stems pulled up from the ground as arrows. Both teams had trash can lids to use as shields to try to protect themselves. My team would walk across the roof of the old, abandoned house, looking through the holes to see if we spotted any of the enemies on the other team. If we saw any, we would throw a dirt clog and try to hit them with it. They would try to retaliate by looking upward through the rooftops to see us and shoot us with an arrow. I realize now that was a dangerous game to play, but we felt that we were invincible when we were young.

So, there I was on the top of the roof when I spotted one of the enemies through a hole. I aimed and got ready to throw and hit him in the back with a tomahawk when suddenly, an arrow came rocketing upward and hit me straight in the center of my forehead. One of my brother's friends who had gotten into some trouble recently had shot me. I quickly yelled, "Time out. I have been shot in the head!" I immediately hopped down to the ground and asked everyone what to do with the arrow sticking out of my head. They said to pull it out. Being young and naive, I broke it off, thinking that I had pulled it out. It bled for a moment and stopped, so we went back to playing. My older brother said, "Farraday, do not tell Mama what happened because we do not want our friend to get in trouble and possibly go to Gates Ville," a juvenile delinquent center.

So, we continued to play until dark and went home. Mom saw the wound on my head and asked me what happened. My older brother gave me a pointed look, so I said we were playing war, and I must have fallen on some wood.

Later, I was having a nightmare, and I was talking in my sleep, saying, "Time out everybody. I have been shot in the head with an arrow." Then I said, "Do not worry, Clarence. I will not tell Mama about our friend because I do not want him to get into trouble." My sweet mom was listening to it all. She had brought me a cold rag because my face was swelling up. The following day my head was as big as a watermelon, and I could barely see out of my eyes. Mom prayed for me first and took off work to take me to the doctor.

The doctor pulled over one inch of stalk debris out of my forehead and said if it had gone a little deeper, it could have caused some brain damage. As we were driving home, Mom said, "Now when we get home, I will ask you, in front of your brother, what happened to your head because I do not believe that you can fall and that much wood could go into your head, son." I got nervous and wondered what to say because I did not like whippings. When we got home, my mom asked me again in front of my older brother.

My older brother gave me that look again. I said, "Yes, I fell, Mom." She told us both that she was going to whip us for lying, and she knew that my brother had been the one to tell me to lie.

She said, "Why would you lie to me after all that I have taught you guys about telling the truth? Don't you know that the truth will set you free? Remember this when you tell a lie, it needs something to stand on, which is another lie, but the truth does not need something to stand on; it can always stand on its own."

There is a fundamental principle to be learned in this situation.

I learned that my response should have been, especially in this case, to tell the truth, and deal with the consequences, constantly praying and asking for the Lord's help. I believe that dishonesty can affect our self-worth because it causes us to see ourselves in the wrong way. Lying can cause distrust in relationships and our society. I now know that it can cause you to catch a whipping too.

Things to think about:
- Lying is not good, and it just starts a web of lies.
- Do not allow intimidation to cause you to compromise the truth.
- Have the courage to stand up for what's right.

Scripture to know:

Ephesians 4:25 (NLT)—Stop telling lies. Let us tell our neighbors the truth, for we are all part of the same body in Christ. Lying disrupts unity by creating conflicts and destroying trust in one another.

Questions for you:

Can you remember a time in your childhood where you have felt pressured not to be honest about something? How did you respond?

_____
_____
_____
_____
_____
_____

Have you experienced a time in your life that you went with the flow of your friends' decisions when you knew it was wrong? How did you feel after you did that?

_____
_____
_____
_____
_____
_____

Lessons in Football

One beautiful Saturday morning, our friends asked if Clarence and I could play football in the park with them. Mom had us do our chores first, and then she prayed for God to protect us as we played and let our lights shine to others.

As we headed to the park, my friend, Gerald, sent me out on a long pass to practice my catching ability before we arrived at the park. In those days, we wore cutoff T-shirts with our favorite professional football players' numbers on them. Lots of kids came from surrounding towns to play sandlot tackle football against each other at this park. I could tell today was going to be an extremely competitive day. We did not have gangs, like the Crips and Bloods in California, but we did have territorial gangs that represented kids from other close surrounding cities, like the west side, the south side, Stop 6, and Lake Como.

My friends and I wanted to be picked for the west side team. Since the older guys always picked the teams, we had to show we were worthy of being on their team. But the whole time, the older guys ridiculed us, calling us weaklings, and told us to give up so they could pick some of their buddies instead. After all, their strategy worked on a few guys who decided that they did not want to play on their team. I became a little discouraged and frustrated from their ridicule until I remembered what my mom always told me about having a bad attitude. She said, "Son, always remember that your attitude will determine your altitude; therefore, always try to maintain a good and positive attitude so the Lord can help lift you."

I also remembered that she had prayed for us before we left the house.

So, I was being ridiculed, and I had to prove I was worthy of playing on the west side team. Remembering that I was a good track star in school, I asked my friend Gerald to throw me a long bomb pass down the field. I dashed down the field like a bolt of lightning as I ran toward the end zone, and I caught the long pass. The other team leaders were looking and were amazed at my speed and catching ability. They all wanted me to play on their team, but the west side team leaders said, "No way, you cannot have him because he is already on our team."

I became a marvelous light to them and the other team players. During the fourth inning of a tied game, with only a few minutes left, the quarterback said, "Farraday, I want you to run a down-and-out play, then run toward the end zone for a long bomb pass." I ran like a rocket blasting down the field. After the play, I headed straight toward the end zone. Gerald threw what we called, at the time, "A Bob Hayes Bomb" down the field, and miraculously, I caught the ball and scored the winning touchdown. My team players were ecstatic, and they picked me up and nominated me the player of the day. I was filled with excitement, enthusiasm, and joy.

Things to think about:

So, what is the teaching or moral of the story as it relates to peer pressure?
- Never allow your peers to intimidate you or tell you who you are as a person.
- Evaluate your position and learn who you are in Christ.
- When making a difficult decision, always try to stay positive and ask for God's help.
- We must remember that prayers change things. My mom's prayer certainly helped me.
- Be responsible for what you can do. (Do not follow the crowds even when some kids quit and give up.)
- God will give us the wisdom we need to be victorious.

Scripture to know:

Philippians 4:13—I can do all things through Christ who strengthens me.

This scripture reminds us that in Christ we can do all things, even though we may want to give up.

Questions for you:

Write about a time in your life when your peers have pressured you.

_____
_____
_____
_____
_____

How did you respond? Did you stay strong, or did you give in to their demands?

_____
_____
_____
_____
_____

The Discovery on the Trail

My brother and I would go and stay with Uncle Bill, a Methodist preacher, and our dear Aunt Charlie Mae, a pure sweetheart of an aunt who loved the Lord. They lived in La Marque, Texas, about thirty minutes away from our dad in Galveston. My friend Button would always come to Uncle Bill's house and play marbles with us on the side of the house, and Aunt Charlie Mae would cook us some good old southern sweet red beans and rice. The good news about staying with Uncle Bill and Aunt Charlie Mae is that our cousins lived just around the corner. My mom's brother Uncle Freeman and my other precious Aunt Eva lived there, and they had four kids, who we could play with.

I will never forget that we were playing with our cousins at Uncle Freeman and Aunt Eva's house when they asked us to go to the store with my cousins. Although we had heard that three rough girls often ambushed other kids on the shortcut route, stealing their candy and money, we decided to take that route. The kids warned that we could run if the girls ever ambushed us because the girls were not that fast.

On our way back from the store, we heard the bushes rumble, and out of nowhere, we were faced with three tall, hardcore, rough girls who were demanding all our candy, groceries, and money. We were startled as we looked at each other's faces and wondered what to do. Joseph, my cousin, remembered what the neighborhood kids told us to do, and he yelled out for us to run. Like a flash of lightning, we all scattered in all directions off the trail, trying to make it safely back home to safety. When we ran off the trail, we did not realize that we were not familiar with our surroundings. We were all scattered apart and running, trying to make it back to Uncle Freeman's house. We ran through until we found a gate to the front streets on the side of the house. I lifted my cousin, who was running with me, over the fence and climbed over. We were both huffing and puffing from complete exhaustion as we were getting closer to the house. We looked up the street and saw Uncle Freeman and Joseph coming our way. *Praise God!!! Help is on the way.*

Joseph was the first to make it home, and he told Uncle Freeman what happened. "Where are your sisters, boy?" He said, "I don't know, Dad. We were all scattered and ran."

Uncle Freeman replied, "I want you to know that under no circumstance is it ever right for you to run off and leave your sisters to fend for themselves, and you mean to tell me you let those kids take your stuff from you? Let us go back over there right now, and you are going to get all your stuff back from them."

By this time, we all had made it back, but we were breathless. We were afraid, but because Uncle Freeman was with us and insisted that we all head back to the trail, we gained a slight sense of confidence. We found the girls still on the trail. Uncle Freeman said, "I want you kids to go and ask for all your stuff back from them." The girls looked over at us and said, "We don't care about your daddy being here with you."

But despite their words, we felt confident with Uncle Freeman with us. My cousins asked them for their things back, and they ended up wrestling with the girls, who fell to the ground. . The girls were crying, and they gave us back everything and apologized to all of us. They said they would not do it again. They ended up shaking hands and hugging each of us, including my Uncle Freeman, because he made us apologize to them. They said, "Nobody has ever stood up to us before."

So, we all went back to the house. My Uncle told us to always stick together when something like this happens. "Remember that a team is always better than an individual." We learned a lot from him talking to us about these experiences. One thing we learned is there is real power in numbers. Uncle Freeman said, "The same way the three sisters had three people who boosted their confidence in winning, the six of you could have stuck together and tried to handle it in love by yourselves. But instead, you guys allowed your fears and insecurities to overwhelm you and cause you to react to your feelings and make some bad choices by running from the problem instead of trying to solve it peacefully. The good news is that no one was seriously injured, and you all are safely home with everything back."

Things to think about:

I had a combination of emotions during this story: insecurity, fear, and unforgiveness. Throughout this story, I felt insecure because I didn't know how to respond to this situation, and I feared how things would turn out. At first, it was tough to forgive the girls who attacked us for no reason, but after realizing the harm it could cause me, I decided to forgive them.

What can you do the next time you are in a similar situation experiencing these emotions? You must remember that your response to them is important. Mom used to always tell me, "Whenever you are faced with trouble, try to pray first and ask for God's help. Then think about what is happening."

For example, when I felt insecure about what to do and what the outcome would be, not knowing which way to run or if I should just wait to see what my cousins did, I could have stopped to gain the right perspective. Seeing it through God's Eyes would have given me the confidence to realize that we had real help. And had I turned to that help; I could have felt confident in my decision. When we put God first in a situation, our enemies begin to get smaller.

Now for fear. We all get fearful in various situations, especially when we do not know what might happen to us. But we should pray first and ask for God's wisdom and help. Fear is the opposite of faith, and we must have faith to please God.

Now let us deal with unforgiveness. Since I was still upset about the situation, I had to consider the consequences of holding grudges and staying angry with them. I have discovered that when I refuse to forgive others, my unforgiveness will keep me emotionally stuck to them and the offense. And if I continue to refuse to forgive them, it can dig an even deeper hole in my heart that can cause a root of bitterness to occur. Therefore, the wisest thing for me is to ask for forgiveness after an altercation like this one.

Scriptures to know:

Proverbs 3:5–6 will help you when dealing with these emotions— Trust in the Lord with all your heart And lean not on your own understanding; In all of your ways acknowledge Him, And He shall direct your paths.

2nd Timothy 1:7(NKJ) reminds us that the Lord has not given us a spirit of fear, but love, power, and a sound mind.

Matthew 6:14–15 (CSB)—For if you forgive others their offenses, your Heavenly Father will forgive you as well. But if you do not forgive others, your Father will not forgive your offenses.

Questions for you:

Have you experienced a time in your life where you were fearful? What happened?

_____
_____
_____
_____
_____
_____

Have you had to really trust God to work a situation out for you and direct your path? What did you do?

_____
_____

The Power of Love

I can remember the wonderful summers when we would go to Galveston and spend the entire three months out of school with our dear dad. Every summer while visiting him, my uncle, aunt, and our cousins, who lived in a nearby town, would have so much fun and enjoy going to church weekly with Uncle Bill and Aunt Charlie Mae. I always looked forward to going to church.

On the way home from one of these fun summers, I thought about how different my mom's relationship with us was from my dad's. Mom gave us continuous hugs and kisses all the time. She also told us that she loved us frequently, while Dad was not much of a hugger, but he would buy us anything that we desired or wanted. He always gave us money to buy school clothes and Christmas presents. Whatever we would ask Dad to do or get for us, he would. So in the car on the way back to Fort Worth, I asked my mom, "Why does Daddy not hug and kiss us or tell us he loves us like you do?"

She replied, "Your dad does love both of you dearly; he just expresses it differently than I do. Your dad lost his mom when he was five years old, so maybe he didn't get a chance to experience getting a lot of hugs and kisses from his mom. So, you guys can teach him how to do that next summer when you go to visit. All you need to do is extend your arms out for him, and he will respond by hugging you back. Then you can help your dad experience how it makes him feel to get hugs and kisses from his sons."

So, the next summer, I couldn't wait to see dad and offer him a great big hug and kiss. Dad was open and very receptive to them both. Eventually, my brother and I got used to receiving them from Dad too. Every time before we would leave to go somewhere with

Uncle Bill, Dad would open his arms wide, expecting to get a hug.

This began creating a real sense of love between us, and my dad wanted us to live with him in Galveston. He told us to think about it. One day my mom set my brother and me down at our kitchen nook and said, "Well, I guess the hugs and kisses worked because I just received a letter for us to go to court because your dad is trying to take you guys from Mama." We hugged Mom as tears flooded our eyes and said, "Never, Mom." We all prayed together and asked God to please work things out for us to stay together.

Since my dad had his own business, he thought it would help him prove to the judge that he was more capable of providing for us than Mom. He was expecting favor from the judge.

When it was time for our scheduled court date, we went to court afraid but knowing it was in God's hands, as we had prayed many times. The judge called my mom up first and asked her to present her work status. My mom told her where she was currently working but was willing to get a second job to keep her kids with her. My dad was next, and he presented income statements, indicating that he had more than enough to adequately take care of us with ease, and he would be willing to pay our mom some extra wages for allowing him to keep us.

The judge said, "Let's get the kids in here and see how they feel." While we were afraid, our mom had prayed with us. The judge asked us how we felt about the matter. With tears streaming down our eyes, we said we wanted to stay with our mom. We knew that our dad loved us too, but he had a business to run, and he had a very limited amount of time to spend and do things with us. We wanted to stay with our mom because mom is more than a mother; she is our best friend. I said, "My dear mom is giving us something that no amount of money can buy, and that is her unconditional love for us and her precious time."

With tears welling up from deep inside, we begged the judge to let us stay with our mom because she is everything to us. When we are sick, she cuddles us in her arms and heals us with her hugs of comfort. She prays with us daily, cooks for us, and even plays sports games with us, like basketball and baseball. Essentially, she gives of herself. The judge almost started to cry herself, and then she said, "We must leave these kids with their mom." It appears to me that she is providing them with all they need, and that is love. She said, "I believe there is absolutely no amount of money that can quench these two kids' thirst for the love they are being given by their dear Mama."

My dear mom was such an exceptionally loving person. She told us not to be angry at Dad. We must forgive him and continue to show him love, for he did not mean us any harm. He has just grown to value love for himself. She added, "But always remember that God is always faithful because of His love for us. Now I want you both to write your dear dad a letter telling him that you forgive him for that, and you will always love him."

Things to think about:

- There is no substitute for unconditional love.
- No amount of money or materialistic things can take the place of real love.
- Spending quality time and listening to your kids can strengthen the bond and express your love for them.
- It is a good thing to try to be involved with your kids' fun activities, especially when they are younger. They will remember those times.

Scriptures to know:

1st John 4:8 (NLT)—But anyone who does not love does not know God, for God is love.

1st Corinthians 13:4, 7 (NLT)—Love is patience and kind. Love is not jealous or boastful or proud or rude. It does not demand its own way. It is not irritable, and it keeps no record of being wronged. It does not rejoice about injustice but rejoices whenever the truth wins out. Love never gives up, never loses faith, is always hopeful, and endures through every circumstance.

Romans 12:9–10 (NLT)—Don't just pretend to love others. Really love them. Hate what is wrong. Hold tightly to what is good. Love each other with genuine affection and take delight in honoring each other."

Questions for you:

How have you experienced the power of love in your life?

___
___
___
___
___

What are some good examples that you can think of to express God's love to your family and others?

___
___
___
___
___

The Power of Prayer

While growing up, I always prayed for a few things: to catch up with my peers in school and for my mom and dad to get back together. I never really understood why they were separated because Mom had given us tremendous love, and when we went to Galveston, Dad would treat us so well.

One thing Mom always told me was that I was as smart as anybody else in my classroom. She said, "We all have the same opportunity to pay attention and learn." Because my birthday was in November, I had to start school at the age of seven, which was a year after my peers, who were six. That made me feel like I was a year behind and created a sense of insecurity because I felt as if I did not have the same opportunity that other kids had.

But when I was feeling down about this, Mom always tried to inspire me, not just with this, but in all things. She would say, "Son, you can be whatever you want to be in life if you put God first and keep striving toward it, giving Him 100 percent and all that you got." That stuck with me as I grew older because I always felt like I was at a disadvantage, being one of the older kids in my class.

When I was in the second grade, I made straight A's, and I wanted to ask the administration if I could skip a grade to catch up with my schoolmates, but my mom wouldn't let me. She thought it would have been too much for me and my little mind.

So I thought that was it. I wouldn't get my wishes. Then, one day my mom called Clarence Jr. and me to a meeting at our kitchen nook area. This was the place that we would often assemble when Mom had something of importance to discuss. She said, "Well our prayers are working. Your dad and I talked for a long time last night. He said he wants us to come and live in Galveston with him." We were so excited, and we could hardly believe it. She mentioned that after we got settled in, he would buy my mom, brother, and me a brand-new home in La Marque, Texas, which was close to our uncles, aunts, and cousins. Clarence Jr., my oldest brother, and I were overly excited in one way, but we felt a little sad because we had built such great relationships with our friends. But Mom always expressed to my dear brother and me how important family is and encouraged us to love each other and always remain close to each other.

So, there I was in Galveston, Texas, and it was my first day of school. They directed me to go to the designated spot for my grade level. I thought about what my mom had always taught me about being as smart as anybody else in the classroom. Although I was scheduled to enter the eighth grade, my transcript had not arrived from Fort Worth, Texas. I decided that since they had three levels for the ninth graders to enter 9A, 9B, or 9C, I would go into the ninth grade and choose 9C, the lower level. This would be my big opportunity to catch up to the right grade level that my peers were in. My mom said all I had to do was pay attention and do what the teacher said, and I could make straight A's. I made straight A's in the ninth grade for two semesters, and after that, my transcripts from Fort Worth finally came in. The principal called my mother to schedule a meeting to discuss this matter. The next day Mom and I came to the principal's office. I explained that I always wanted to catch up with my peers who started school when they were six years old, and I had to start when I was seven. This situation always made me feel insecure and disadvantaged because I felt that I was falling behind. I prayed about it and decided to enter the ninth grade in my new school. God was so good and faithful because since I had made straight A's in the ninth grade, thanks to my mom, they decided to give me an eighth-grade equivalency test, and I passed it and remained in the ninth grade.

God was truly faithful, and I began to realize the power of prayer.

Things to think about:

- God is so faithful even when sometimes we are so faithless.
- There is real power in prayer.
- Prayer really can change things.
- Never give up on your prayers.

Scriptures to know:

Mark 11:24 (NKJ)—Therefore I say to you, whatever things you ask when you pray, believe that you receive them, and you will have them.

Philippians 4:6 (NKJ)—Be anxious for nothing, but in everything by prayer and supplication, with thanksgiving, let your requests be made known to God."

Questions for you:

Have you ever prayed for God to do something for you during your childhood? How did that work out?

_____
_____
_____
_____
_____

Have you ever prayed for God to help you with a situation occurring in your family? What happened?

_____
_____
_____
_____
_____

Love Never Fails

My dad spoiled me in the tenth grade by buying me a nice car to drive to school, and my friend Chip Mills taught me how to dress sharp since my dad often gave me extra money. I felt on top of the world with my car and clothes.

But even better, I finally was able to enroll in an art class in the eleventh grade, and my instructor Mr. L.T. Gordon was a tremendous influence in my life. I won several awards in ceramics and painting. He also helped me to get a scholarship to go to college at Texas Southern University.

After a few years in college, I started hanging out with new buddies I had met in school. We would often meet up and go to another college campus down the street and attend live entertainment concerts and after-parties. At the parties, I was introduced to all kinds of drugs and alcohol. Eventually, after attending a few of the concerts and after-parties, I started drinking and using drugs. Then, through one of my friends, I was introduced to what I thought was the "good life." I learned about the hustle and bustle of street life and planned to make a lot of money selling drugs, then I would go back to college.

During those years, my dad had lost his tavern business, and afterward, God had changed his life. My dear dad would often minister and pray for people in his neighborhood. Everybody would come to him for prayer, advice, and encouragement. His nickname was Do Boy. People knew Do Boy would help them, feed them, and extend some words of encouragement to them. They knew God had profoundly changed my dad's life because he used to be a real gangster when he was running a tavern in a rundown neighborhood. Since God had changed his life, I would often stop on this street corner where Daddy started hanging out to chat with him. There was a mailbox right there on that corner, so I would give Daddy money to help him since he didn't have his business anymore, and he was helping others. Looking back, I probably tried to help him because I also felt guilty about what I was doing. Every time I would give him money, he would take it and put it in a pre-addressed envelope to Oral Robert's Ministry, Trinity Broadcasting Network, and other TV ministries. He would say, "Son, I'm sending up seeds for you because Daddy is praying for you, and I know God is going to bring you out of that lifestyle you are in right now." I would ask him not to give the money to the TV ministries because I wanted him to have it. But he wouldn't keep it. He said, "You can keep your money because it is all the devil's money, but if you're giving it to me, I'm going to send it up to Heaven through these ministries and believe that God is going to bring you into His family of believers because I'm dedicating that money back to God for His good purposes on your behalf."

One day I was following a few friends in my car to go and do a transaction when my dear old dad waved me down. I told the guys, "That is my dad, so I got to stop and see what he wants." When I pulled up, Dad ran over to the car and said, "Look, what they sent to me for you." It was a beautiful Gold Leaf Bible with my name inscribed on it. I said, "Dad, I love it, but I can't take it today. Hold it for me, and I'll come and get it later." That stayed on my mind for the rest of the day.

All I could remember was seeing Dad's enthusiastic smile and the glittering in his eyes as he was trying to give me that Bible. Several weeks later, what I thought was the easy way of life was becoming a nightmare because a lot of the guys who were selling drugs for me on the streets were getting busted, and things had gotten a little hot for my drug supplier and me. Therefore, I couldn't make any money. It appeared that the heat from the police was getting close to me. So, I ultimately decided to go and pick up my Bible from Dad after these bad occurrences had happened. I also finally took my mom's advice, went back to church and work, and stopped selling drugs.

When I went back to work, I was kind of embarrassed because I was used to what I had considered, at the time, the good life. During this period of my life, I learned an especially important principle: God will often have to break us of our self-pride to help bring us back to reality.

After I cleaned up my act, my first job was working for the City of Galveston in the sewer department. On my first day at work, while riding in the city work van, a few guys were whispering to each other about me being that big-time dope dealer on the streets. I would wear my dark shades to disguise myself, especially when we would make stops in areas where others knew me from my previous lifestyle.

One day after work, my mom asked me what was wrong. I told her I would quit this job because I had to go to an area where I used to hustle, and I felt funny that these guys saw me working for the sewer department. My mom said, "Son, can't you see that is nothing but self-pride? And by the way, God hates self-pride, and that is probably one of the first areas that He is targeting in your life that He wants you to change." Mom told me to let go of my pride, to humble myself, and learn to be thankful that God has brought me out of that lifestyle. She said, "And besides, many of the other guys who saw you probably wish they were in your shoes and had your job. They probably want the Lord to turn their lives around too.

"Now, tomorrow when you go to work, Mama wants you to pray first, pull those shades off, and be proud that God has given you that job, and He is giving you another chance in life to become the person He is calling you to be."

I thought, wow, Mom seems to have this special spiritual insight to see my situation from a different perspective. She always knew what to say to get me back on track.

Things to think about:

In this story, I dealt with self-pride, peer pressure, and insecurity. Being spoiled by my parents and living the "good" life contributed to my sense of pride. But we should never forget that it is God who supplies all our needs, and we should learn to stay humble and thankful and practice having an attitude of gratitude and thanksgiving. We should never think more highly of ourselves than we ought to. While the drug life provided me with money, what I thought was the sign of success, it didn't help me grow as a person, which is truly the sign of success. We should strive to learn how to allow God to help us. It is always wise to have an intelligent, spiritual friend, one who you know will be honest with you and tell you the truth. And in my case, it was my mother.

Street life also brought about a feeling of insecurity. Discontinuing my college classes made me feel insecure because I was no longer looking in the direction of what I could become by being educated. Life became unmanageable, and I had begun to lose my sense of hope for my future. We should pray for God's help and allow Him to direct us out of our dark situations and come to our senses. We should strive to get back on the right track.

Then, of course, I felt pressured by my peers who knew me as a big-time dope dealer. Luckily, my mom steered me in the right direction of not worrying about what others say.

In humility, I am grateful God gave me another opportunity first to change directions.

Scriptures to know:

James 4:6 (NLT)—God opposes the proud but gives grace to the humble.

1st Corinthians 15:33 (NLT)—Don't be fooled by those who say such things, for bad company corrupts good character.

1st Corinthians 13:8,13 (NKJ)—Love never fails . . . And now abided faith, hope, love, these three; but the greatest is love.

Questions for you:

When have you felt pride getting in your way? What were you prideful of? How were you able to humble yourself before the Lord? Or, if you are still caught in pride, how can you humble yourself?

_____
_____
_____
_____
_____

Have you ever been involved with the wrong type of friends and got into trouble? What happened? How did you get out of it? Or how can you get out of it?

_____
_____
_____
_____
_____

Part 2:
The Sapling Level— (Developing Stage)

Often we must venture through several roads in our lives to reach our full potential in God. That was certainly the case for me.

Prayer Changes Things

One cool day while working at the water pump station in Galveston, I received a call from Shirley, an old flame of mine that revolutionized my entire life. I was given a new sense of hope and determination. It was real love from the very start. We talked on the phone on and off during our shifts at work, with her being in California on her job and me being in Texas on mine. This communication continued for at least six to eight months.

During that time, because of my drug usage, I lost the water pump station job, but I had started regularly working on different construction jobs.

Shirley and her son, Marquice, moved to Texas, and Shirley and I were happily married. After the church ceremony, we meandered down the streets in a horse and carriage, headed to the famous Galveston Strand.

The only problem was even though we were married and loved each other and God dearly, we were still torn and broken vessels who had experienced some hurts, negative habits, hang-ups, and emotional scars in our lives.

I had previous experiences of the hustle and bustle of street life, but I was trying to turn my life around and settle down and learn how to enjoy family life. I often attended N.A. and A.A. meetings, and I attended church weekly to learn how to live life on life's terms. For several months, we lived together and tried to get familiar with each other and our everyday lives. I applied for another job at the water pump station in Texas City, Texas, where we had been looking for our dream house. The job looked very promising at first. When it was down to me, and one other applicant, my dear wife and I prayed. We asked Him that if it was His will to allow me to get that job so we could move to Texas City and raise our family, then to help make it happen, and if it was not His will to please close the door and allow us to move to California and start our new lives together.

While my wife and I were reminiscing on our beautiful future of being together, we saw a cement bench on the seawall and sat on it. We hugged and snuggled up together and held up one of our hands, each outstretched toward the sky, and prayed for God to please use us and our ministry that He would give us in California. We had no idea why that prayer had come out of our mouths. Well, as promising as the job in Texas City at the water pump station looked, I did not get the job. So, my sweet wife and I started the process of making plans to move to California.

My wife and I asked God to order our steps and give us the wisdom and knowledge to make this transition to California possible. We also prayed for God to teach us more about Him, so we could eventually do His will in California.

I moved in with my mom while my wife, who was pregnant at the time, and Marquice went to California to look for an apartment to live in. Moving to California created a sense of insecurity in me because it was a big challenge. It appeared like I had to get ready to leap over tall mountains to reach my purpose and destiny in life.

The Sapling Level— (Developing Stage)

My lawyer friend, Mr. RA Apffel, said, "Son, I think that California would be great for you and your new family. I think because you are an African American, you will be treated more fairly in California because they have progressed more, and I think there will be greater opportunities for you there. I will tell you this one thing, I know for sure, California will either make you or break you, because they will treat you like a real man out there." Immediately I thought about my mother and what she told me when I was a little kid growing up: "Always remember that you can do and be anything you desire to be as long as you put God first and keep striving forward as you give Him one hundred percent and all that you got."

I continued to pray to God daily to supply me with the funds to get us an apartment in California. God was so faithful; He gave me enough construction work and even overtime to quickly get enough money to pay for the deposit and the first month's rent, despite the high rents in California.

Though I was excited, I was nervous about leaving the security of having my parents nearby. But, with their encouragement, I launched into a new adventure that would be filled with belief, trust, and an incredible faith in God. So, I said my goodbyes in Texas, and I headed to California to fulfill the destiny that God had set for my new family and me.

Once my plane landed at the airport, my heart fluttered with joy and excitement to see Shirley, Marquice, my new mother-in-law, sister-in-law, and two brothers-in-law. They greeted me at the airport. I was overwhelmed with great anticipation. I arrived on a Thursday night, and they had already filled my weekend and the whole next week with activities to help me get to know California.

So, after the wonderful week of showing me beautiful California, it was time for me to start seeking work to provide for my dear family.

Now I was in a place where the rubber meets the road. I had to believe the Word of God for what it said and believe that God can do what He said He can do. Well, at that time, just being here was a real miracle.

Shirley's sweet mom had given us a car so that I could look for work. I prayed daily with my wife before we went to Manpower and other work agencies to apply for work. I needed anything available to be able to pay my next month's rent. God was faithful, and after a few days, I got a call to go and help a man do lawn work for a few weeks. I said, "Praise God."

My brother-in-law James drove me to the lawn care job. I grabbed my lunch and excitedly went out to greet the owner. He said, "I hope you don't mind listening to this gospel music because that's all that I listen to." Of course, I loved it. This job was an answered prayer. I explained to him who I was and what my goals were as far as taking care of my pregnant wife and Marquice here in California. He said, "God is faithful, and He will help you take care of your family."

I told him that I had just moved from Texas a week before, and I had only paid my deposit and my first month's rent, but I had faith in God. I told him that I had been praying to get a job with benefits and put in applications daily. He immediately pulled over to the side of the road and prayed with me, and he asked God to please answer our prayers and continue to meet our every need. We continued our journey to cut the lawns. The town we entered was so ritzy and luxurious to me, with pristine and well-kept yards and large swimming pools in the backyard. We blew the leaves into piles, put them into plastic bags, and loaded them on his truck, easier work than I had done in Texas. This was a great day for me. He even kept me an extra three weeks as we waited patiently on God to answer our prayers.

Well, God did give me a great job with benefits at CMS Welding and Machining Company in the shipping and receiving department. The lawn man was extremely happy for me. Things were going great, and I was able to add my family to my insurance.

The Sapling Level— (Developing Stage)

Things to think about:
- Prayer can change your life
- You should learn to be patient and wait on Him
- You need to learn to trust God, for even when you don't get an answer right away, it doesn't mean He isn't listening.

Scriptures to know:

Psalm 4:1 (NLT)—Answer when I call to you, O God who declares me innocent, Free me from my troubles. Have mercy on me and hear my prayer.

Psalm 69:13 (ESV)—But as for me, my prayer is to You, Oh Lord. At an acceptable time, Oh God, in the abundance of Your steadfast love answer me in Your saving faithfulness.

Questions for you:

Have you experienced a time in your life when you prayed to God, and you had to learn to trust and wait on His timing for your answer to your prayer? Did you have patience? Did it all work out?

_____
_____
_____
_____
_____

Have you ever stepped out in faith to accomplish a mission that seemed to be impossible to do in your own strength? What happened?

_____
_____
_____
_____
_____
_____

The Road to Transformation

One day while driving, I received a call from my job's dispatcher saying I needed to rush to the hospital because my wife was in labor. I was driving as fast as I could to get to the hospital, but when I got there, it was too late; Farrah had already been born. I was so thrilled and excited to see it was a baby girl. My coworkers celebrated with me the next day.

Now that we had two kids, I felt a deeper sense of responsibility. Stress built up, and I began to feel insecure, wondering if I could provide for my family as I should.

I once heard a pastor say, "Where the mind goes, the man or woman follows." One day while I was driving and thinking about where I was in my life and my concerns, I lost my focus, and a car rapidly stopped in front of me, causing me to rear-end them in the company's truck. I thanked God that no one was seriously injured, but I still had to go to the doctor to ensure I was all right. The doctor felt I shouldn't go back to work for a while. This added even more stress for my dear wife and me.

When stress built up, I would revert to my old drinking and doing drugs to handle things. These character defects and abusive behaviors caused havoc in my relationship, resulting in our separation. We had scheduled a counseling session with Pastor Tony to help us get through this phase of our lives. My wife and kids stayed a few days with her mom before we went to our counseling session. The pastor had us write down ten things that we wanted to gain out of our marriage—our expectations of the marriage. When I arrived at the church, I was excited and eagerly holding the list of my ten expectations for our marriage. When my wife and precious kids drove up to the church, the kids ran out of the car saying, "Daddy, we missed you!" and they gave me a great big hug. I was overwhelmed with joy. Little did I know that I was about to experience a rude awakening.

Shirley and I went into the pastor's office, and the kids were sent to the kid's nursery. We sat down, and Pastor Tony asked if we had

The Sapling Level— (Developing Stage)

done our homework. Feeling excited, I volunteered to read my list first. I talked about the vision and expectations that I had for our marriage.

When it was Shirley's turn, she said, "Pastor, I've decided that for now, all I want is child support until my husband deals with some of his character defects. To be really honest with you, it's going to take a miracle to put our marriage back together." The pastor looked at me very grimly and said, "I'm sorry, Brother Farraday, but we can't go any further with these counseling sessions since this is where Shirley is now. Let's pray."

I felt wrecked because I had prayed, and I wanted to be given another opportunity to work things out for us. I walked out of the office with tears falling down my cheeks as I watched my dear wife and precious kids walk away. They all gave me one last big hug.

I was so emotionally bewildered, not knowing what to do. The pastor said, "Brother Farraday, please don't go anywhere because I want to talk to you, but first, let me walk your wife and kids out to their car."

After he returned, he invited me to go for a drive with him.

He told me, "Son, we are co-laborers with God, so remember that without God, we can't; but without us, He won't because we are in this thing together with Him."

I replied, "I made the list, but she wants to leave me! Did you hear her say it will take a miracle for us to stay together?"

The pastor broke out laughing. "Please don't take this personally, Brother Farraday, but I am laughing because you don't get that the God we serve doesn't want to do *small* things in your life. The miracle is His greatest work. That is what He does best, the miracle!

"But first, He wants to work on you and get you prepared to receive your family back, and that process starts with you because you can only change yourself. Shirley needs to see that change in you, my dear brother. And the good news is, I know firsthand that this can happen because He changed my life.

"So, let us pray and allow God to start His total transformation process in your life. I want you to know right now, it is not going to be easy, and you will have to go through a few things, but the good news is that our God will walk you through it all, and He will never forsake you or leave you. And in the end, you will come out much wiser, stronger, smarter, and fit for the master's use."

Things to think about:

It is amazing how I can now look back over my life and realize that God was still right there during everything. Our God loves you so much He wanted me to share some of my trials so you could know that no matter what you have been through or are now going through in your life, God is willing and able to help reestablish you in Him. We must always remember that God is determined to make us whole if we pray and ask Him to.

No matter what you may be facing right now in your life, God is right there with you to supply you with what you will need to reach your full potential in Him. Remember, you are God's workmanship, created in Christ Jesus for good works, which He prepared beforehand that you should walk in them.

Scriptures to know:

2nd Corinthians 5:17 (NKJ)—Therefore, if anyone is in Christ, he is a new creation; old things have passed away; behold, all things have become new.

Philippians 4:6, 7 (NKJ)—Be anxious for nothing, but in everything by prayer and supplication, with thanksgiving, let your requests be made known to God, and the peace of God which surpasses all understanding, will guard your hearts and minds through Christ Jesus.

Philippians 4:13 (NKJ)—I can do all things through Christ who strengthens me.

Matthew 6:33 (NKJ)—But seek first the kingdom of God and His righteousness, and all these things shall be added to you.

The Sapling Level— (Developing Stage)

It is amazing how even during the raging storms in your life, God is still right there with you. He will help you through your dilemma if you acknowledge and ask Him to.

Questions for you:

Can you remember the time in your life that God started transforming you?

_____
_____
_____
_____
_____

Have you been excited about celebrating something special, and then our spiritual enemy showed up and tried to bring havoc in your life? What did you do?

_____
_____
_____
_____
_____

My Wilderness Journey

Well, since my alcohol and drug use had caused my separation, there I was with nothing but God to hold onto. I was blessed to still have some income coming in from being on workman compensation. But I was forced to learn how to survive in California without my wife and kids by my side. I had to endure my loneliness, insecurity, anger, pain, and fear. This was when I began to understand that Our Lord and Savior is so real. I prayed daily and asked Him for guidance.

Being separated from my dear wife and kids made me feel like a real failure in life. My sense of security was also shattered because

Discover The Real You

I couldn't work. I had lost my sense of focus and could not think about anything but being with my family.

During this time, my mom would call me regularly to pray with me and make sure I was all right. My mom said, "Son, you are more than welcome to come back home to Texas and try to get yourself together, and I will do all that I can to help you accomplish that. But I know that if you ask God and give Him a try, He will see you through this." She always knew exactly what to say to get me fired up and strengthen my faith in God. Her words of encouragement always helped me to keep striving.

Things to think about:

Just like her words of encouragement, I would like to cheer you on to continue this inspiring journey with me as I learn how to walk by faith and not by sight. One day at a time, you too can learn that God will walk with you through every situation or circumstance you may face. We must remember that He is faithful even when we are faithless.

In the next section, we will see how God led me step by step in developing a personal relationship with Him.

Let us pray:
Father God, I thank you for whoever is reading these stories in this book, and I pray that you would supernaturally touch their hearts, no matter where they may be in their lives. I pray that you would speak peace, healing, and restoration in their lives and journeys, right now in Jesus's mighty name. Please help them with the transformation process in becoming whole again. We thank you because we know that You love us and have our best interest in your mind. Amen.

Scriptures to know:

Proverbs 3:5, 6 (NKJ)—Trust in the Lord with your whole heart And lean not on your own understanding; In all your ways acknowledge Him, And He shall direct your paths.

2nd Corinthians 5:7 (NKJ)—We walk by faith, and not by sight.

Isaiah 26: 3 (NKJ)—You will keep him in perfect peace, Whose mind is stayed on You, Because he trusts in You.

Questions for you:

Can you remember having a wilderness journey in your life? What happened, and how did you respond?

_____
_____
_____
_____
_____

Did you have anyone to listen to you and encourage you during your wilderness journey? Who was it, and what did they do for you?

_____
_____
_____
_____
_____

My Faith Journey

Since the lease was in Shirley's name, I could not keep the apartment, and I found myself homeless. I had to put my clothes in storage and find living quarters. I prayed for the Lord to give me a place to stay that night. I found out about a shelter for people experiencing homelessness called the Armory in San Jose. So I went and stayed there for one night. I was sad because of my position, but I was excited because I always wanted to see and feel how homeless people felt and think. They were just like me; they all had a story to tell.

I filled my time there by drawing pictures of people and giving them the sketches afterward. They were happy to receive my gift, and it helped me assist others instead of dwelling on my situation. I was astonished that one night of living there could provide me with the strength and courage I needed to continue my journey. The Lord revealed to me how blessed I was compared to many other homeless people I met that night. It made me humble myself and thank the Lord for my daily provisions. I still had a place to shower, eat, change my clothes, and have an income more importantly!

When morning came, I read my Bible and then left. I prayed again and asked God to please give me a place to stay at least for a week. I talked to a few members after church, and they sent me to The City Team Rescue Mission. I went there, and I told them my situation and who my pastor was. They eagerly accepted me into their daily living program as long as I promised to abstain from all drug usage, clean up around the mission, go to Bible studies, and be in at a certain time. They had two weeks available.

After the two-week period was up, I prayed again and asked God to please give me a place to stay where I could have more privacy to spend time with Him. The next day one of the church members told me about a lady nearby who had lost her husband and had a room for rent. She needed the extra money to help pay the mortgage. The price was within my small budget, so I moved in with only a small deposit and the first month's rent. After a week had passed, some of her relatives moved into town, so I had to move out. So, I talked to some people in the church, and they recommended another lady who had a room for rent. She also was in desperate need of money, and I was desperate to find a place. Of course, I did not stress as much this time because I could go back to City Team Rescue Mission because my pastor was well known there. I could tell that God was developing my trust and faith in Him by showing me that He was walking with me daily through every situation and circumstance. At times, I let my fears get the best of me and delay my progress. But then I would remember the words of my mom and put my faith in God. He was teaching me more about His faithfulness, for He would never forsake me or leave me. God also showed me that He would meet my daily needs. Through it all, my mom would call and pray with me daily. She always poured lots of faith and love into my heart. Just hearing her voice uplifted me.

As I checked the new room and living conditions out, it seemed the Lord was teaching me how to trust Him for my daily provisions.

The Sapling Level— (Developing Stage)

During the daytime, the lady who owned the home appeared to be fine. She spoke kindly, and her attitude was pleasant. But she would often play her music loudly and party with her friends at night. She would always try to invite me to come in and have some fun with them, but I politely would decline and go back into my room. The only thing that I had not noticed was that she had burglar bars on all the windows where you could not get in or out without going through one of the doors. One night I was in my room listening to some praise music when I heard a banging sound on my door. She was tripping on alcohol and drugs, calling me names, and cussing me out through the door. She kept saying that I thought that I was better than her and her friends, and that is why I did not want to party or socialize with them. I prayed and asked the Lord to help me and show me what to do. I decided not to respond to what she said and just asked her to stop banging on my door. She eventually stopped.

The next morning she asked me to forgive her for her disruption the night before. She also promised me that it would not happen again. Wow! I had only been there one week, and I was already beginning to have problems. I had already paid a deposit and one month's rent. I prayed for another place to stay because I had not planned on having these types of problems. I told Brother Dee, a great friend of mine and a mighty prayer warrior, what had happened. I asked him to please be on the lookout for another room to stay in if this continued to happen. He agreed to help me and add me to their prayer list.

The next weekend, the banging and name-calling continued. And again, the next morning, she apologized. I tried to do the right thing by informing her that I was in the process of inquiring about another place to live because things were not working out for me here as I expected.

Well, my friend Dee called me and said that his friend told him about another place with rooms for rent. Two other brothers who lived there also attended the church and Bible studies. I thanked my landlord but told her I was moving out next week.

After that, I sensed that she was upset because she did not say much to me. I told her not to worry about returning any money because I knew that could create a bigger problem. Besides, we went to the same church.

That next morning I praised God, meditated on His Word, and thanked Him for the new place to live. When I went to shower, she politely tapped on the bathroom door and said, "I'm leaving now because I have some errands that I need to run."

When I opened the bathroom door, I noticed the front door was locked, so I could not go out of the house that way. But when I decided to go out of the house through the back door, I noticed a child's protective gate blocking the pathway to get out. When I reached to open the protective gate, two large Rottweilers jumped up, barking and trying to bite me. It frightened me to death. I almost panicked when I remembered what my mom told me to do if I ever get in trouble: always call on the Lord, especially when you have a desperate need.

So, I rushed back into my room, got on my knees, and immediately started to pray. The Lord brought Dee to my mind, and I gave him a call, and he said he would come by and get me. This was one of my most powerful experiences of the real power of God being manifested in my life. Dee made it to the house and informed me that he was waiting outside the backdoor. He told me I had to get out of the house before she came back, but I was afraid those dogs would bite me. He said, "My brother you have to pray to God, and He will protect you and tell you what to do. I will also be out here praying for you, but you have to get out because I have to go to work soon. It was nobody but God who had me at home for this purpose."

Once I finished praying for protection from the dogs, I was led to go and move the gates open and head to the back door. When I passed through the gate, God's Glory and His manifested power were magnificently demonstrated to me because when the dogs started to come toward me, they suddenly howled, backed up, and

The Sapling Level— (Developing Stage)

covered their faces with their paws. After making it out, my friend asked what had happened with the dogs. I was still overwhelmed by what had just happened and didn't think he would believe me.

He told me we could call the police tomorrow. He had a dear friend who is a police officer.

The next day God was faithful, and I could get my things out, including my bicycle, and move to the other room that God had already prepared for me. This time I had a few cool church brothers to pray and collaborate with. I knew the Lord was steadily walking with me through it all. God was beginning to exhibit how real He is.

Things to think about:

So here I was stuck on this merry-go-round concerning my future living conditions, but God was unquestionably still walking with me day by day throughout it all. Though my situation seemed dismal, He kept providing various solutions to give me time to fix it on my own. He doesn't magically make your problems go away, but He provides a way for you to get out of the situation if you put your trust in Him. You, too, might be facing a trial in your life that seems to be a little foggy, and you cannot see your way. I want you to know without a shadow of a doubt that we must depend on God to see us through.

At times in your life, others of lack faith can harm you. During these times, you must learn how to create boundaries and distance yourself from them to avoid being hurt. Always try to have at least one or two faith-filled friends who you can call on, especially for prayer, wisdom, or help.

Never doubt the power of God in your life. He will strengthen you as you go through different trials to prove how much He loves you. Then you can put your total trust and faith in Him as you continue your journeys and keep walking by faith in His glorious plan for your life.

Scriptures to know:

Hebrews 11:1 (NKJ)—Now faith is the substance of things hoped for, the evidence of things not seen.

Hebrews 11:6 (NKJ)—But without faith it is impossible to please Him, for he who comes to God must believe that He is, and that He is a rewarder of those who diligently seek Him.

Isaiah 41:10 (NKJ)—Fear not, for I am with you; Be not dismayed, for I am your God. I will strengthen you, Yes, I will help you, I will uphold you with My righteous right hand.

Psalm 37:23 (NKJ)—The steps of a good man are ordered by the Lord.

Questions for you:

Can you think of a time when you had to learn how to put all of your faith and trust totally in God? What happened?

_____
_____
_____
_____
_____
_____

Have you ever experienced a time in your life where you were in a desperate situation, and you had to pray to God to seek help from others? What happened?

_____
_____
_____
_____
_____
_____

Why do you think it is very important to develop a routine of spending time with God daily in His Word and prayer?

The Sapling Level— (Developing Stage)

Walking by Faith Part 1

So, here I was on my third stop in my housing journey, and I was getting stronger in my faith, wiser in my thinking, and smarter about this God who was walking me through these unbelievable trials. Clearly, God really was observing me and walking with me through my trials. He ordered my steps to strengthen me and get me to my destination gradually while I learned how to trust Him on new levels. With my strength renewed in God, I knew I could get myself back together. I started attending church and Bible study more often now that I had roommates who had cars and did not mind taking me along with them. We often prayed together and talked about God.

As I attended Bible study, I learned more about God. For over a month, I had been riding my bicycle to the bus stop, then to the Bart station, then to San Francisco, then walking past a park, and then going to another bus stop to go to the doctor. From that car accident, I had a back injury that required weekly therapy visits to monitor my progress. My weekly assessments were also required for me to get my workman compensation money. Luckily, I hadn't had any problems. God was walking with me daily and teaching me more about Him. He was teaching me that I could stand flat-footed on His Word and promises. He was teaching me that He would take good care of me as long as I continued to learn to believe, trust, and obey Him.

I would ride my bicycle over ten miles just to try and peep at my kids at my mother-in-law's house. Now and then, Shirley and my precious kids would meet me at an eating place, and I would hug them and buy them food. I would often stop and pray on the side of the road, asking the Lord to develop me to be the man he wanted me to be so I would be worthy of getting my kids back, even if my wife and I didn't get back together. I knew deep in my heart the Lord heard my prayers. While my faith had increased, I knew the Lord had more work to do to transform me. He had to help me tear down my many negative behaviors, such as letting my emotions overwhelm me by feeling stressed and angry at my situation. The only way through this was to really cast all my cares on Him and stop taking it back into my own hands. To do this, it was important to continually study His Word as often as possible for my inner strength and peace. Learning to trust God for my daily needs was very essential.

Now and then, I would run out of money until my check would come in the mail. One day I had to go to the doctor, and I did not have enough money to catch Bart. I barely had enough to catch the bus. Our Bible study for the week was about God supplying all our needs according to His riches in glory. We had to believe it to receive it. So, I was almost to the Bart station but with no money for the ticket, so I prayed to the Lord, asking Him to meet my every need according to His riches in glory. Usually, I would lock my bike on the bicycle rack. But this time, it seemed like the Lord wanted me to go somewhere else before I locked up my bicycle. I said, "Lord, I hope this is you leading me to ride up this street." I was always at least thirty to forty-five minutes early. So, I rode my bicycle two blocks, and I had no idea why, but as I rode by the park, a guy came up to me and said, "Will you pray for me?" I said, "Sure, I loved to pray for people because God has so many people praying for me during my journey." I prayed for the guy's specific need, as my Bible study brothers had taught me to do. He thanked me so much for that. He said, "Man, I felt that prayer." Then as I was heading back to the Bart, the Lord led me to stop at the corner and look to the right on the ground. There it was: a twenty-dollar bill on the ground with nobody in sight. I almost cried from being so excited. I caught Bart, and I had extra money to eat too.

The Sapling Level— (Developing Stage)

I made it to San Francisco, went to the doctor, made it back to my bicycle and my bus stop, then safely home to my room. God was teaching me little by little that I can truly trust and depend on Him. If I did His work, He would take care of my needs. I remembered praying for that guy, and I now realized that was the reason that I had an uneasy feeling in my spirit when I began to lock up my bike, even though I did not have the money to catch Bart. I did not know if God wanted me to ask someone for the money or not, but I did sense that He was going to show me what to do. I had peace about the situation because I looked back at all the past victories that God had brought me that were way worse than this one. This is the pathway that God chose to reveal Himself to me. He was also revealing one of my spiritual gifts to me, but at the time, I didn't know about spiritual gifts. I have since learned that I have a gift of faith and prayer.

But even though I was learning these lessons, I still struggled at times, as we all do. See God must often prepare you to receive His blessings. At times, I would get my check, and a sense of self-pride would set in. I would meet my wife and kids at a restaurant, even knowing I could not afford it. Even though I knew I needed the money for other things, I would try to impress them. God had to break that self-pride in me and bring me back to reality.

I can remember one other time that I had mismanaged my money because I overspent it when I would go and see my precious kids. This time it was not by much, but it caused me to not have enough money again to catch the Bart train. I had enough money to ride the bus, but I did not have enough money for the Bart ticket. I was six dollars short. When I reached the station, I got off my bicycle as usual, and I went to go and lock it up in the bicycle rack, hoping that God would send me on perhaps another journey to find the money, but this time, He did not. He wanted me to see that it was my own doing that I was short, and He wanted me not to allow this to happen again because He had provided me with enough money from my check. So instead of praying for the money for the Bart ticked, I prayed and asked Him to help me and please forgive me. I know He was listening to my prayers.

Well, it was getting close to the time to catch the Bart, and I still did not have the money. I said, "Well, Lord, I've done everything that I know to do, and I have run out of solutions of what to do, but I sure need to see my doctor this week for me to continue to get my checks." It was five minutes before the time to go, and I could not see any money on the ground, and I did not see anybody to ask for the money or anything. But I put my trust in the Lord. I pleaded with Him and said, "Lord, you have never let me down. Please help me, Lord. Please, Lord, I won't let this happen again, I promise." Then suddenly, I could sense Him leading me to look at another ticket machine again, and God supernaturally shot a roundtrip ticket out of the machine to me. I was so overwhelmed with joy, and I said, "Lord, I will do anything that You tell me that You want me to do!!!"

So, now I had a roundtrip ticket and extra money for food because I was only six dollars short of having enough to purchase the roundtrip ticket before God blessed me. I made it to San Francisco. When I walked through the park, I could sense the Lord telling me to stop and pray for a few homeless people; then, he led me to feed a few of them from McDonald's near the bus stop.

I learned an unbelievably valuable lesson that day about prioritizing my finances and being more responsible in my obligations, and that never happened again. I learned to leave my money for my weekly expenses and bills at home whenever I went to see my sweet wife and kids at a restaurant. God's patience was extraordinary with me.

Things to think about:

If you find yourself, like me, with misplaced priorities in your life, remember that obedience is the key to the supernatural manifestation of God. I had misplaced my priorities by trying to put impressing my family before my main necessities in life. If you want God to move supernaturally in your life, I double-dog dare you to obey Him. When we obey Him because of our desire to, it tells Him that we do

The Sapling Level— (Developing Stage)

love Him. He says if you love me, you will obey me and my Father who is in Heaven will love you the same way that He loved me, and I will manifest Myself to you.

What I love about God is He will do it all in love. At times, I had to learn the hard way that there are real consequences when I make the wrong choices, no matter what the reason is. God was trying to teach me how to stand up, be strong, and deal with life on life's terms. If the money I had was for my rent, I had to learn how to say, "No, I'm sorry, but Daddy can't do that today." I was so glad to see them and be with them until I felt compelled to say yes to them. I also learned that when I was weak and made the wrong decisions, I was prolonging the Lord's transformation process and prolonging the time it would take to be in a position to receive my family back. But even when we make a bad choice or mistake, God is the only one who can take our mistakes and work them back into our lives for our good and His glory. Romans 8:28 is a good reference scripture for this.

If God is trying to teach you something in the first grade of your learning process, He will not pass you until you pass the test. The good news is that He will give you many times to take it over and over until you get the message and pass it; at least, that is how it was in my life.

- God had to teach me to put first things first, such as food, clothing, and shelter.
- God had to teach me how to trust Him and believe Him and His precious Word.
- Our response to the situations always reveals our faith and what we believe, regardless of what we say.
- God must get us ready to receive His blessings. No matter what you have gone through, or no matter what you are now going through, our God wants to heal and restore you to become whole again if you get a burning desire to know Him. Everybody's story is different, but our God is the same today, tomorrow, and forever, and He loves us unconditionally.

Therefore, I pray that God would speak peace to everyone reading this book and give you wisdom, strength, and the knowledge of how to keep pressing forward through every obstacle that tries to hold you back.

Lord, we know that You can do exceedingly, abundantly, above all that we may think or even ask.

We thank you in advance, Lord, for walking with us by faith, step by step, and we know that You will get us to our proper destination at Your allotted time. We promise that when it is all over, and all the smoke has subsided, we will be quick and very careful to give You every bit of the praise, honor, and glory that is due to You. In Jesus's mighty name is our prayer. Amen.

Scriptures to know:

Hebrews 13:8 (NKJ)—Jesus Christ is the same yesterday, today, and forever.

Ephesians 3:20 (NKJ)—Now unto Him who is able to do exceedingly, abundantly above all that we may ask or think, according to the power that works in us.

Philippians 4:6–7 (NKJ)—Be anxious for nothing, but in everything, by prayer and supplication, with thanksgiving, let your request be made known to God, which surpasses all understanding, will guard your hearts and minds through Jesus Christ.

Questions for you:

In what ways have you felt God's presence in your life?

_____
_____
_____
_____
_____
_____

What spiritual gifts has God given you?

_____
_____
_____
_____
_____

What has God been trying to teach you that you still must learn? What misplaced priorities do you have?

_____
_____
_____
_____
_____

Walking by Faith Part 2

So here I was doing fine, as I had established a weekly routine that seemed to be flowing well: I would attend Bible study, go to Sunday Service, then go to men's monthly fellowship. I was praying daily by myself and with the other brothers in the morning before we went on our different journeys. I prayed and asked God to please give me my own place to see my kids regularly and maybe have them over for a few hours. I had the church congregation, my friends, and my men's monthly fellowship also praying for me concerning finding my own place. I learned to thank God for doing it before it even happened because in doing that, you are expressing your faith and trust in Him.

One morning, one of the brothers was going to pick up another brother to go to Bible study with us, and he asked me to ride with him to pick him up. When we went by there, I noticed that it seemed to be a nice area. I felt led to go and find out how much a studio apartment cost. The landlady said she required references and a credit check.

The devil kept trying to tell me that my credit was bad and none of the people I lived with before would give me a good reference. At that time, I really had not learned a lot about spiritual warfare and how Satan will try to tear you down when you are on the right path. God will teach you and give you what you need to continue the faith journey that He is taking you on. This day at Bible study, the message was twofold: the pastor was beginning to start a series on spiritual warfare, but the real message for today was to know that absolutely nothing is too hard for our God to do. I felt surprisingly good.

So, I prayed and thanked God in advance for the apartment. One morning Dee called me and came by and picked me up. We prayed together, and he took me to eat breakfast. He was a real example of a consistent prayer warrior who did not just talk the talk but walked the walk. After a nice breakfast, he made sure that I was doing okay in my thinking.

After breakfast, we went to a men's fellowship, and the message was about forgiving others to position yourself to where God could open His windows of Heaven and bless you. After the men's fellowship, my friend began to tell me that he felt the Lord leading him to tell me to forgive my coworkers and to go back to work. I said, "You know that is so funny because I was thinking the same thing after that message."

I was still upset with the management on my job because it seemed like they did not want to talk to me since I had been off for so long. So, I prayed, and I decided to go and talk to the management department at my old job. I had been off for over a year. I first went in and asked to have a meeting with the management staff. I told them the reason I wanted them all there was because I wanted to apologize for my negative attitude and behavior since I had been off. I said, "Will you all, please forgive me? I am now ready to come back to work if you would allow me to, and I promise to be safe, be here on time, and give my job 100 percent."

The Sapling Level— (Developing Stage)

They were somewhat reluctant, and they left the room to discuss the matter. When they came back in, they said, "Okay, when do you want to start?" I said, "I already have my doctor's release, and I would like to start right now if possible." Since they were really busy in the shipping department, they told me I could start work there. I went to work with so much joy and enthusiasm. They noticed how great my performance and attitude were and asked me if I minded working a few hours of overtime. They noticed that when I left that I was on a bicycle. So, after I left, they sent their driver to go and offered to give me a ride home.

I began to pray daily and ask God to please give me my own place. After two weeks of working, I was led to ask one of the guys who lived in one of the rooms to please take me to the apartment where we picked up his friend for Bible study. I wanted to ask them about this apartment again now that I had a job. I had asked before this, and the apartment manager said she couldn't lease me an apartment based on a check from the workman's compensation since it wasn't completely disability pay. I had told the lady the last time that I was separated from my family and kids, and I really missed them, and I just wanted a place to call my own so they could come and visit me. She admired that I was a dad who really loved his family and was trying so hard to see them. When I told her I had a job, she informed me she had one studio apartment left, but they went fast. I said out loud, "Lord, please help me." She said, "I love the Lord too. I will call one of my Christian sisters who works for the Red Cross and explain to her what's going on and see what she says." I said, "Can we pray about it now before you call her?" She said, "Of course, we can." So, we prayed and asked God to give me His favor in this situation. She said, "Well, give me your phone number, and I will give you a call tomorrow and let you know how it went with her." I gave her my phone number and went back to the room to prepare to go to work tomorrow. Everyone was praying for me. I was so excited until I could barely sleep that night.

During my lunch break at work the next day, I received a call from the lady from the apartment. She said God heard and answered our prayers, and He exceeded our expectations. Not only are they going to pay for your deposit, but they are also even going to pay for your first month's rent. All I need you to do is give me the twenty dollars to run your credit check. She said, "We're going to help you see your kids because kids need a father figure in their lives." I started crying, but this time it was tears of joy. This was another incredible miracle that God had performed. I was totally ecstatic and overwhelmed with unspeakable joy!

Things to think about:

As you continue with me on my journeys of walking in faith, I want you to know that prayer is very essential to help you stay focused on God.

My church brothers who lived in the house taught me to pray for specific needs and to thank Him in advance, even before He answered my prayers because this would show my faith and belief in Him. When you do this, the devil is going to always try to bring up your past failures, problems, or something negative to try to get you to doubt God. In my case, he tried to bring up the fact that my credit was not good, and my prior landlords would not give me a good reference. To help you combat the devil, keep attending church and Bible studies, and always try to fill your mind with God's Word and promises for your life. Start to believe that all things are possible to those who believe, trust, and obey God. And please remember to always monitor your thought life and the words you say because you want to always try to stay positive and speak life to yourself and others.

Scriptures to know:

Mark 10:27 (NKJ)—But Jesus looked at them and said, "With men it is impossible, but not with God; for with God all things are possible."

Jeremiah 32:27 (NKJ)—Behold, I am the Lord, the God of all flesh. Is there anything too hard for Me?

The Sapling Level— (Developing Stage)

Roman 4:17 (NKJ)—I have made you a father of many nations. In the presence of Him whom he believed God, who gives life to the dead and calls those things which do not exist as though they did.

1st. Peter 5:6 (NLT)—So humble yourselves under the mighty power of God, and at the right time He will lift you up in honor.

Questions for you:

Has there been a time in your walk of faith that the devil tried to bring up bad things about your past or tear you down in some way? How did you respond?

_____
_____
_____
_____
_____

Why do you think it is important to pray specific prayers to God about your situation? What will the results be?

_____
_____
_____
_____
_____

Why do you think you should thank God in advance for answering your prayers? What does that tell Him about your faith in Him?

_____
_____
_____
_____
_____

Having Faith in God's Promises

Our Lord has given us many promises through His precious Word concerning our lives. God said in the Book of Joel that He would restore the years that the cankerworms had stolen from His children if they would repent and come back and bring Him their sins, shame, and problems. He would redeem and restore them. Just like He did for them, God will turn your past hurts, negative habits, and hang-ups into weapons that you can use to help others for His glory.

God was faithful, and I moved into the apartment. I was so excited and thrilled to see that God had faithfully given me a place to call my very own. I continued to work, and I started to see my kids regularly. Shirley would drop them off to be with me for several hours. Often, I would take them to the Discovery Zone Center to play and eat, as it was two blocks away from me.

We always had so much fun together, and I learned how to spend quality time with my dear kids. I constantly gave them tons of hugs and kisses and told them how much I loved them, just like my mom taught us to do with our dad.

One day while riding my bicycle home from work, I saw an old Lincoln Continental car for sale. I stopped to see how much the man wanted for the car. He wanted seven hundred and fifty dollars. The owner was an older retired man who lived alone because his wife had passed. I told him part of my amazing testimony about how good God had been to me by giving me a place to stay and then being able to see my kids. I asked if I could give him two hundred dollars to hold the car for me. He showed me papers where he had the engine rebuilt, tuned up, and oil changed regularly. Although I knew it would take me a while to pay for it, I had prayed to God for transportation. After paying the two hundred down payment, I could only give the man fifty dollars toward my purchase for the next month. He said, "I've had many people come by and offer to pay me all of the cash for the car right now, but for some reason, I have felt led not to sell it." I said, "Sir, I know you may need your money right now, and if you decide to sell it, I won't be upset, and

The Sapling Level— (Developing Stage)

I will understand." He assured me that if he sold it, he would give my money back. Amazingly after two weeks, the car was still there. I said, "Lord, I need that car, so please help me to get the money to get it." The next week I passed by the man's house, and he looked all excited and seemed to be waiting on me to pass by on my bicycle. He asked me to go with him to the DMV. As we headed to the DMV, he said, "I couldn't sleep well last night, and you and your family kept coming to my mind. I don't know if it was the Lord or what, but all I know is that I need to fill this car up with gas, change the paperwork at the DMV, and get you two months of liability insurance in your name and give this car to you with the balance owed being a gift to you, and we can call it even."

The Lord had shown Himself to be faithful once again in my life. I prayed with the man, and I gave him a great big hug. He invited me to come and visit him with my kids sometimes. I did take them to visit with him occasionally. I am not exactly sure why God had chosen this man and situation to reveal Himself to me in a more intimate way, but He did.

1st Peter 5:7 (NKJ) says, "You can cast all of your cares on Him, for He cares for you."

Father God, I pray right now for everyone who is reading this message for you to help them with every need that they have in their lives. I pray for the renewing of their minds to understand the hope of your calling for them. I pray that they would be supernaturally strengthened by your mighty power and be able to find their purpose in life and do the things that you have appointed them to do. I pray that you would heal and restore any broken relationships and mend all broken hearts in Jesus's mighty name. Amen.

So here I was now with my very own studio apartment, and God had given me a car to go to work in. I prayed daily to the Lord, thanking Him for the many blessings that He was continuing to bestow upon me. I began to develop a weekly routine of going to work, Bible study, and church. And I was more involved with my family, taking my kids shopping at the malls with Shirley to buy them clothes and out to dinner regularly.

I would like to pause for a moment and speak to any younger person reading this book or anybody who has not learned the importance of learning how to make a budget and learn to live within your means. Life seemed to be going well for me, but I had not learned how to budget yet; therefore, when it would come time to pay my monthly rent, I would be short on the funds. I think I had to pay a couple of late fees before I realized that I had a money management problem. I can remember on one occasion I took Shirley and the kids to some special event, and I ended up spending all my rent money, but we had a marvelous time. I wanted to be back with my dear family so badly. After the event, everybody was full and happy, and Shirley and I communicated well with each other throughout the day. When I went up to my apartment, I found a note on my door from the manager saying she needed to talk to me. I worried because I knew it had to be concerning my rent being late. I prayed to the Lord to please help me and tell me what to do. The next morning instead of passing in front of the office to go to my car in the parking lot, I was afraid, and I went down the back stairway and went around the whole apartment building to avoid being seen.

I never will forget the situation because God spoke to me all day through several messages on the radio. His message to me was that I could trust Him in all situations to help me. He said, "But first, I want you to quit running from your problems and learn to deal with them by facing them head-on and be honest and look for Me to show up in it. Do not be afraid because I have promised you that I will never forsake you or leave you." Wow! After about four different messages from different pastors on the radio, I began to understand what God was telling me to do in this situation. So right after work, I went to the office to talk to the landlord, and I told her the truth about what had happened. She said, "I've been watching you and your wonderful kids, and I can see how badly you want your family back. I have a few apartments that you can clean up for me to get ready so I can rent them out, and that will take care of this month's rent for you. And if you're interested, I might have a few others for

The Sapling Level— (Developing Stage)

you to help me get cleaned up to rent out for you to deduct some money from your rent each month." With tears of joy streaming down my eyes, I gave her a great big hug. She said, "You just keep doing the right thing, son. I believe God is going to give you back your family in due time."

I wrote about this incident in my praise report journal. I had learned to keep one now, for me to see what God was doing in my life. I prayed and thanked God for helping me learn how to face my problems head-on, trusting Him while looking and expecting Him to show up in it. I also asked Him to please help me learn how to manage my money better. I needed to learn how to take care of myself and my kids properly. Well, the Lord answered my prayers by sending me my dear cousin Larry Jordan. He drove from Oakland, California, over fifty miles away, on a special trip to help me develop a budget and to help me determine exactly what my problem was concerning my finances. After evaluation, I learned that I was spending over five hundred dollars a month on amusement with my wife and kids that I could not afford. So, Larry helped me set up a weekly budget.

Along with a clear weekly budget, I needed to get a loan to pay off my excessive credit card debts, or I had to get a second job and get back on track. Larry and I prayed together and asked for God's direction and help for me. I did not have anyone from whom I could borrow the money, so my only option was to get an additional job. I thanked my dear cousin for helping me to see exactly where I was and what I had to do. From this, I learned how to put first things first and still enjoy my kids on a limited budget.

I put in several part-time applications at different places. There was a grocery store next to the apartments where I lived, and there was a laundromat downstairs that was privately owned. One day I went to the store, and I felt led to stop at the laundromat to see if they needed any part-time help. The owner was a Christian and said she could give me twenty hours a week and prayed with me to restore my family. God was so faithful.

Things to think about:

During this experience, I was insecure because I could not clearly see what I was doing with my money without a budget. Therefore, I would just spend my money trying to satisfy myself and my kids without prioritizing my bills. The way to respond if you are faced with a similar situation is to always pray first and ask for God's help. He will give you the wisdom needed to make the correct and wisest decision concerning your situation. In my case, it was to learn how to create a budget, sacrifice, prioritize things, and get a second job.

I had self-pride in the sense of thinking that I could spend and do as I pleased because I had a job, not realizing that I needed to learn how to prioritize my spending and create a budget. I want you to always know there are always consequences to the choices that you make in life.

Maintaining a humble attitude allowed me to be honest with myself by admitting that I needed help from Larry. I was so grateful to him for making himself available to me for that entire day at his own expense.

I want you to know that no matter what insecurities you may be facing in your life right now, our God can help you learn how to place all your insecurities on Him and his love for you. He will give you the courage to face any trial or situation in your life. He can do exceedingly, abundantly, above all that you may think or even ask. Everything you ever need can be found in Jesus.

Scriptures to know:

James 1:5 (NKJ)—If any of you lacks wisdom, let him ask of God, who gives to all liberally and without reproach, and it will be given to him.

Proverbs 3:5, 6 (NKJ)—Trust in the Lord with your whole heart and lean not on your own understanding but in all of your ways acknowledge Him and He will direct your path.

1st Peter 5:6 (NKJ) comes to my mind in this situation because

The Sapling Level— (Developing Stage)

God says, "Therefore, humble yourself under the mighty hand of God, that He may exalt you in due time."

Ephesians 3:20 (ESV) says—Now unto Him who is able to do far more abundantly than all that we ask or think, according to the power that works within us.

Questions for you:

Have you experienced God fulfilling some of His promises to you during your faith journey?

_____
_____
_____
_____
_____
_____

Has God ever surprised you by blessing you through others unexpectedly? If so, why do you believe He did that?

_____
_____
_____
_____
_____
_____

Have you ever been led down a specific pathway by God only to meet the right person at the right time to be a blessing to you? What happened?

_____
_____
_____
_____
_____
_____

Interlude:
Your Turn

During my sapling level (developing stage), I had to release past hurts and let go of my negative habits and hang-ups as I learned to walk in faith. You, too, need to release past hurts and change your negative habits before you can discover the real you.

Releasing Past Hurts

Have you experienced some hurts in your life that seem to haunt you causing you to relive the pain, hurts that refuse to go away, no matter what you did? Maybe it was from verbal or physical abuse. Maybe hurts from childhood memories that seem to resurface in your mind.

Well, I have some good news for you because if you apply these practical methods consistently in your life, you will learn how to release your past hurts and start to head toward a life of freedom, fulfillment, and victory as you learn how to reach your full potential in God and begin to discover the real you.

Step one: realize that you cannot do it on your own and will need God's help.

So, I want to pause for a moment and have you repeat this prayer to be assured that you have God's helper to assist you.

Dear Lord Jesus, I know that I am a sinner, and I ask for your forgiveness. I believe you died for my sins and rose from the dead. I turn from my sins and invite you to come into my heart and life. Please save me. I want to trust and follow you as my Lord and Savior.

Now that you have asked the Lord to save you and to help you, you now have a real helper: the Holy Spirit who will guide you, lead you, strengthen you, comfort you, and help you to overcome and release your past hurts.

God has given us many promises as one of his kids to stand on and believe.

James 1:5 (NKJ) says, "If any of you lacks wisdom, let him ask of God, who gives to all liberally and without reproach, and it will be given to him."

Lord Jesus, please give me the wisdom to be able to release my past hurts and be able to press forward toward the life of freedom and victory that you have promised me, in Jesus's mighty name. Amen.

Step two: acknowledge the hurt and pain that exists. There may have been times when you have tried to handle them yourself by denying the hurt or pain, stuffing it, and pushing it deep down inside. Unfortunately, this will prevent you from dealing with it, and often it will keep you stuck in a rut in that area of your life.

It may also resurface at the wrong time. However, when we acknowledge the hurt and pain, we can freely give it to God and begin to deal with it.

Job 5:11 (NKJ) says, "He sets on high those who are lowly, And those who mourn are lifted to safety."

Isaiah 41:10 (NLT) says, "Do not be afraid, for I am with you. Do not be discouraged, for I am your God. I will strengthen you and help you. I will uphold you with my victorious right hand."

Step three: focus on allowing God to change you, realizing that you can only change yourself. You cannot change others.

Romans 12:1–2 (NLT) says, "And so, dear brothers and sisters, I plead with you to give your bodies to God because of all he has done for you."

Let your body be a living sacrifice to Him—the kind He will find acceptable; this is truly the way to worship Him.

Do not copy the behaviors and customs of this world, but let God transform you into a new person by changing the way you think. Then you will learn to know God's will for you, which is good and pleasing and perfect.

I love the way the NKJ translation expresses those verses in Romans: "We must not be conformed any longer to this world, but be transformed by the renewing of your mind, that you may prove what is that good and acceptable and perfect will of God."

2nd Corinthians 5:17 (NKJ) says, "Therefore, if anyone is in Christ, he is a new creation: old things have passed away; behold, all things have become new."

Your old life has passed away, and now you can begin a new life with the help of the Holy Spirit. God wants to help you get rid of all your past hurts and for you to keep striving forward toward the great life he has prepared for you.

Step four: be aware daily of how you are thinking. You should learn to think positive thoughts about others and yourself. The renewing process mentioned in the previous step starts with learning who God says you are as His child. Then you should ponder on those things. For example, God says in these scriptures:

Psalms 139:14 (NASB) "I will give thanks to You, for I am fearfully and wonderfully made; Wonderful are your works, and my soul knows it very well."

Philippians 4:13 (NKJ) "I can do all things through Christ who strengthens me."

Romans 8:37 (NKJ) "Yet in all these things we are more than conquerors through Him who loved us"

Philippians 4:8 (ESV) "Finally, brothers, whatever is true, whatever is honorable, whatever is lovely, whatever is commendable, if there is any excellence, if there is anything worthy of praise, think about these things."

Step five: watch what you say to yourself and others. You should always try to speak life to yourself and others.

Proverbs 18:21 (NKJ) says, "Death and Life are in the power of the tongue, And those who love it will eat its fruit."

Our tongues can bring joy or can cause misery for ourselves and others. Our words can either speak life or death. We should use our tongues and words to build others up and not tear them down. We should learn how to express our feelings to each other without placing blame on each other.

I want to share something that I found to be extremely helpful for me during my transformation process:

You should use an "I statement" to express your feelings to others. When you use an "I statement," you should always remember to tell them about your expected outcome to know how to respond the next time to keep peace and enhance your communication process.

Example: I feel _____ [describe the hurt feeling in the blank] when you_____ [describe the action in the blank]. I wish you would _____ [give your preferred behavior results for the next time in this blank].

Real example: Let us say a spouse feels afraid or disrespected. They could say to their partner, "When you yell or talk loudly to me, I feel afraid, I wish you would talk in a lower tone the next time so we can communicate better with each other."

Please try it because I find it especially useful in communicating my feelings to someone without placing blame.

Never use "you statements" because they always place blame on the other person. In this case, the person always directly feels the blame accusation, which will often stop or hinder the communication process.

Example: "You make me_____ [the offense in the blank]."

Step six: always try to have at least one close friend you can talk to who supports you and will not blame you. Someone who will allow you to vent to them so you can release some of your pain by talking it out. Someone who will be truthful with you and not allow you to get stuck in self-pity. A friend who will listen and encourage you to deal with the pain and keep you moving forward as you discover the real you.

Proverbs 18:15 (ESV) says, "An intelligent heart acquires knowledge, and the ear of the wise seeks knowledge."

Step seven: forgive the offender when possible and yourself.

This is an especially important step to take to help you release the hurt from your heart.

Matthew 6:14–15 (ESV) says, "For if you forgive others their trespasses, your Heavenly Father will also forgive you, but if you do not forgive others their trespasses, neither will your Father forgive your trespasses."

Here is a practical step that I have learned from many ministers.

When possible, without creating any problems, ask the person to forgive you for the wrong you have done to them. If this isn't possible, maybe the person cannot be there, or it could create a bigger problem for you, then you can do it in the Holy Spirit's presence. To do this, get two chairs and place them, so they are facing each other. Sit in one and imagine the other person is sitting in the other.

- Exercise your will by asking the Holy Spirit to help you forgive.
- Ask the Holy Spirit to help you to release them from all debt that you feel they owe you.
- Say out loud, "I declare and decree that you are set free from all past hurts that I have incurred from you."
- Now, thank the Holy Spirit for helping you to do it through prayer.
- Prayer: I thank you, Holy Spirit, for helping me to forgive _____ [Say the name of the person in the blank], and I choose to release [name of person] from all debts and hurts done to me. I ask that you allow me to take back all the ground that the enemy has taken from me. Right now, I give that territory back to You, Lord Jesus. I thank you for hearing my prayers and helping me through this process in Jesus's mighty name. Amen.
- You should also put your name in the blank and forgive yourself.

Step eight: pray and ask the Lord to give you a professional faith-based counselor who can help you go deeper in removing perhaps some strongholds that may be deeply rooted in your subconscious mind. The Holy Spirit will lead you to the proper help.

Lord Jesus, I come to You in the humblest way, and I thank You right now on credit for allowing me to be able to forgive and release the past hurts that have happened to me in my life. I cast all of my cares and hurts in my heart upon you, and I know I am healed from them all in Jesus's mighty name. Amen.

Releasing the Negative Habits and Hang-Ups

Are there some negative habits and hang-ups in your life that you are constantly struggling to stop? Do you self-sabotage yourself with negative words at times? Do you need to be right and perfect all the time or have a need to please people? Are you always trying to control everything and everyone to make sure you will not get hurt again and continuing to ride what seems like a continuous merry-go-round? Are you constantly running from your problems, like I was at one time, instead of dealing with them and confronting them head-on in Christ Jesus?

Well, you may have these negative habits and hang-ups in your life that hold you back from God's amazing promises and blessings, but I know our awesome God's power can set you free and help you to release the negative habits and hang-ups in your life as you discover the real you.

What you are facing has a real spiritual problem. Your human efforts alone cannot solve this problem because your problems have spiritual influences involved in them.

Therefore, you need to follow these practical techniques that I have used to help me release the negative habits and hang-ups in my life with God's help.

Step one: make sure that you have your spiritual helper from Jesus Christ to assist you. We must realize that we cannot do it with our own strength and power.

So, first, I want you to make sure that you have accepted Jesus Christ as your spiritual Lord and Savior through prayer. Then you will have access to your spiritual helper, who is the Holy Spirit.
Dear Lord Jesus, I know that I am a sinner, and I ask for your forgiveness. I believe you died for my sins and rose from the dead. I turn from my sins and invite you to come into my heart and life. Please save me. I want to trust and follow you as my Lord and Savior.

Step two: admit that you have negative habits and hang-ups that are not good for you. You should always consider the negative consequences that are related to them.

Step three: ask your helper, the Holy Spirit, to give you the knowledge and wisdom to help you release these negative habits and hang-ups.

The Holy Spirit may lead you to join a small group to help you be with others who are dealing with similar negative habits and hang-ups. The support and knowledge gained can be awesome, at least it was for me.

Step four: join an accountability group or attend A Celebrate Recovery Group, a Christ-centered program developed and founded by John and Cheryl Baker born out of Saddleback Church with Pastor Rick Warren, where you can begin to apply your faith with others and gain spiritual insight as to how to overcome and release the negative habits and hang-ups in your life one day at a time.

Step five: allow God to help you create a spiritual plan. In your accountability groups, you can develop a spiritual plan by jotting down information from each topic discussed, implementing the information you are learning daily, and evaluating your progress monthly. Several Celebrate Recovery study books address specific needs. After you find a group, regularly discuss your meetings, go through the books, and allow God to help, you overcome and release your past negative habits and hang-ups.

Step six: continue to pray daily and ask for God's guidance through His Holy Spirit, taking it one day at a time. Spend time around positive people and make sure you have some short-term and long-term goals. A short-term goal can be a goal you want to achieve anywhere from now up until a year. For example, in the next four months, I want to finish studying, discussing, and implementing one of my Celebrate Recovery study books. In the next two months, I want to learn and share some of what I am learning in my accountability group. These short-term goals can help you create effective strategies, stop procrastination, and provide you with good feedback from others. A long-term goal is a goal that can take years to accomplish. It has an objective that you want to accomplish in the future. For example, within the next two to three years, I want to become a counselor to help others with their struggles in addictions and other areas of their lives.

You must keep striving and pressing forward toward reaching your full potential in God and begin to release the negative habits and hang-ups as you continue to discover the real you.

Part 3:
The Blooming Level (Maturing Stage)

God's Restoration Process

Now we continue on another courageous and adventurous journey as we discover how God kept helping me mature into the person He was calling me to be as He restored my precious family during His restoration process.

According to Webster's dictionary, *restoration* means the action of returning something to a former owner, place, or condition. The biblical meaning of this word means to receive back more than had been lost to the point where the final was greater than the original was. Essentially, tremendous improvement had been made. Well, this is exactly what the Lord had done for me. God restored me and my precious wife, Shirley, and my two kids, Marquice and Farrah. God not only restored my marriage, but He also gave us a brand-new home in Madera, California.

After a few years of living together and enjoying our lives with our wonderful kids, we continued to attend church, do Bible studies together, and do things together on the weekends. At the time, I was commuting to San Jose, which was a three-hour drive from where we had purchased our home. I would leave early Monday at 2:30 a.m. to get to work at 6 a.m., and I had to rent a room during the week. This was truly a tremendous sacrifice for me, but I felt it was well worth it. We continued to pray and thank the Lord for our restoration process. One weekend Shirley and I had finished doing a Bible study together, and we decided to take the kids to the mall for a treat and a small outing. While in the mall, Shirley said, "Look at these beautiful paintings." She knew I was an artist, but at the time, I had put my passion on hold to make sure I was focusing on my family first. I looked at the paintings and said, "Wow, look at that amazing and radiant light." Shirley said, "It's funny you said that because he is called 'the painter of light.'"

When we returned home, I wrote in my praise report journal about the wonderful experiences we had at the mall. I also thanked the Lord for giving me His glorious inspiration from the beautiful paintings. Those fabulous paintings inspired me to pick up my brushes the next week and paint some. Shirley and the kids were so thrilled to see me back in my art studio room painting again.

After a few weeks, I got a call from Larry McGill, a dear friend and coworker, who invited me to his church in Campbell, California, a three-hour drive. Larry said he wanted to introduce me to this famous artist who spoke that day at his church. I agreed to pray about whether I should go, and in the end, Shirley and I both felt that I needed to go. Little did I know that once again, God, through His Holy Spirit, was guiding me and leading me toward the purpose and plans He had for my life. When I walked into the foyer of the beautiful church, I immediately saw artwork everywhere. One of the paintings was the same one that Shirley had shown me in the mall. It was by Mr. Thomas Kinkade, the painter of light, and Larry knew him personally because they went to the same church.

So he introduced me to Mr. Thomas Kinkade and told him that I was an aspiring artist. Mr. Kinkade said, "Hello, Farraday, glad to meet you. You will have to come over to my company and see what all we do there, and maybe you might be interested in joining my team of artists." Several weeks later, I applied for a part-time job with Mr. Thomas Kinkade's company in San Jose, California. This job would require me to travel mostly on the weekends to different states, and eventually different countries, to demonstrate Mr. Thomas Kinkade's technique to his collectors, tell them interesting stories about him and his family, and personalize the images for them by allowing them to choose specific areas that they wanted me to enhance for them. During my interview, the woman said, "I've never interviewed a person with this much enthusiasm, joy, and energy." I explained to her what getting this job would mean to me. It would be like God making my dreams in life come true. Well, I was given the seal of approval that day by three different supervisors and managers. They said they felt that my enthusiasm and excitement would be good for the position and the company. Well, our Lord had supernaturally blessed me again with an amazing job that would allow me to see the country and represent one of His servants, Thomas Kinkade. My supervisor at my other job was so astonished I would be working for Kinkade that he was willing to be flexible with my work schedule so I could take advantage of this once-in-a-lifetime opportunity.

Traveling Ambassadors of Light Adventures

Since this is a part of my blooming level and maturing stage of my life, I want to share a few of the many adventures that God gave me while serving as one of His traveling ambassadors of light (what Thomas Kinkade called us) and master highlighters for Mr. Thomas Kinkade. Many other sensational events occurred, but because of the space in this book, I can only mention a few.

I always prayed and asked for God's blessing to be on the shows before I went to my master highlighting events, which consisted of demonstrating Mr. Thomas Kinkade's technique on one of his images, spending fifteen minutes with each collector personalizing the image for them, and telling stories about Kinkade and his wonderful family. I also helped them find the hidden Ns in the images—he hid them for his childhood sweetheart Nanette, who was his inspiration for creating the painting.

One particular show was hosted by this extraordinary gallery owner named Mr. Darrell Taylor in Seattle, Washington. We had an awesome, successful day. Darrell and his wonderful family treated me to an exciting and delicious dinner in the Space Needle at the Sky City Restaurant, a five-hundred-foot high-rise building with a rotating glass floor.

This was a very exceptional night because as we reviewed the highlights of that day, Darrell noticed an airplane circling the Space Needle. It had circled three times, at least, before he called our attention to it. "Look, there's a long banner hanging behind it." The banner said, "Will you marry me, Mindy?" We wondered who Mindy was, and our waitress told us Mindy was sitting next to the window and hadn't noticed it yet.

Then suddenly, Mindy looked up, saw the banner, read it, and started crying. We all yelled over to her and said, "Well, will you marry him, Mindy?" She screamed and said, "Yes, yes, yes, I will marry you!" and he put the ring on her finger.

The Blooming Level (Maturing Stage)

We all clapped our hands and congratulated them. God had not only blessed us with a fantastic show but also a great unique incredible ending filled with excitement, joy, and love.

At another event with gallery Owners Al and Susan Fulchino, I mingled with a group of very skillful staff members and some wonderful collectors in Nashua, New Hampshire. New Hampshire is known for its vibrant fall colors. Normally, the highlighting events were hosted at the galleries where the master highlighters would perform and demonstrate Mr. Kinkade's techniques to the collectors. But what made this event so astonishing was that Mr. Thomas Kinkade, himself, was going to be there to speak to the collectors and create a unique sketch on the back of some of the paintings to be silently auctioned off. Since the galleries were too small to hold Mr. Kinkade's personal appearance, Al and Susan had to have the event in Massachusetts in the Lowell Memorial Auditorium. This was a very picturesque place, with a beautiful lake and fall colors glowing all around it. It was a beautiful day, and everyone was excited about the event.

Al set a goal for us to sell over sixty images during the event, and we sold completely out of everything we had, which I believe was over eighty images. The evening was amazing, as we had beautiful Italian music playing, plenty of food, beverages, and we superseded Al's expectations. We completely sold out of all images we had. The Lord blessed us so much, and I even ended up staying a few extra days just trying to finish up all the paintings to be highlighted. God was once again so faithful. We prayed together and thanked the Lord for such an amazing three-day event.

One momentous event was held in New York City. The gallery owners had been preparing for this particular event for weeks and tried to choose the right number of paintings to sell during this occasion. Well, I prayed, as usual, before flying to the event for God to bless the show and to please give us His supernatural favor in the mall.

The weather forecast did not look good for us, which caused great stress and concern for the gallery owners. On the day of my travel to New York, it was snowing profusely when I arrived that evening. Since my plane was delayed and the limousine driver had problems getting through the snow to pick me up and drive me to my hotel, the gallery owners were concerned I wouldn't arrive in time. They were also concerned about the next three days of our scheduled events. The forecasts had predicted snow for all three days.

When I arrived, I called the gallery owners to let them know that I had safely arrived at my hotel. I wanted them to know not only was I safely in, but I was in a great mood; I was anticipating and expecting God to give us a great weekend. The gallery owner said, "I sure hope you're right, Farraday, because I have a lot of money tied up in this event. Tomorrow we can at least do some of the pre-sold images for the event where the collectors will not be present." I prayed with the gallery owner on the phone, and I told him that I knew God was listening to us and I would see him in the morning after breakfast. I woke up that morning an hour early to pray and spend some quality time with the Lord. I asked Him to please help us through this day and please bless us with His supernatural favor, despite the bad weather conditions. The gallery owner picked me up, and I could see and sense his anxiety concerning today's event because it was snowing heavily, and it did not seem like it was lightening up any.

We slowly made it to the Palisades Mall, and from the weather conditions and snow on the ground, the gallery owners were expecting absolutely no sales. I asked them to set me up to highlight the images because I knew God could do something good for us that day. He told me the parking lots were empty, so not to expect much.

I said, "I hear what you're saying, but I have my eyes and my mind fixed on Jesus and what He can do and will do for us despite these conditions."

Mark 9:23 (NKJ) says, "Jesus said to him, "If you can believe all things are possible to him who believes."

The Blooming Level (Maturing Stage)

So, he set me up in the mall, and I highlighted some of the paintings. I had finished highlighting probably four images when I saw a gentleman carrying a walkie-talkie on his side pass by.

He said, "Young man, what are you doing?" I invited him to sit down with me for fifteen minutes during our highlighting sessions. As I highlighted the image, I told him exciting things about Mr. Thomas Kinkade, his painting technique, and his hidden initials in his images. The man was astonished to see how when I added the paint to the images, they began to glow and come to life. I allowed him to choose a few areas for me to highlight. He said, "Son I've never bought any paintings before, but where's the gallery?"

Little did I know that God was getting ready to perform a real miracle for us. The man went to the gallery, and the gallery owner was able to sell that one man over twenty thousand dollars of artwork.

The gallery owner had tears of joy in his eyes. He absolutely could not believe what had just happened. God performed a real miracle for us through this man, who, by the way, was the owner of the plowing company that was moving the snow from the Palisades Mall's parking lot.

The weather conditions changed the next day, and the snow cleared up, so the mall was crowded, and we had an incredible show and a phenomenal weekend.

God had a purpose and a plan for that snowy event. Because of this incredible miracle that God had performed in what seemed to be an impossible situation, I was able to lead the two gallery owners and their friend to the Lord.

No matter what obstacles you may be facing now or have faced in your life, I want you to know that God is real, and He is no respecter of persons. What He has done for me and others, He will gladly do the same for you if you give your life to Him. He will do the impossible, if necessary, to show you His love for you and His desire to make you whole again.

Family Meetings

Everything was going well: I was regularly working for the computer chip industry, traveling all over the country almost every weekend for my art job, and going to a wonderful studio twice a week in Danville, California, where God had blessed me to find a wonderful mentor, an incredibly talented artist named Mr. Charles H. White.

At the studio, I also met Mr. Mitch Neto and Mr. Eric Rhodes. Mr. Mitch Neto is now displaying his work in various gallery studios in California. Mr. Eric Rhodes has now become a renowned magazine publisher, traveling all over the country hosting several of his art business workshops, popular magazine events, and his other successful business seminars. These men have made a tremendous impact on my life. Under my mentor's tutelage, I sold many paintings. He taught me how to better develop my compositions, create great designs for my paintings, and mix wonderful harmonious colors.

Yet, with everything going on in my life, I found myself drifting from my original intent and priority to nurture and provide for my family's needs. So, I was led to create family meetings to help my wife with the kids and school. Since I was traveling so much, I realized I was missing out on too much, so I cut down to only two shows a month, allowing me to spend at least two weeks of quality time with my dear family.

After September 11th happened, one of my goals was to help prepare my kids for their future by using these family meetings as a tool to teach them reading, writing, and arithmetic. I also wanted to teach them how to develop a closer relationship with God to reach their full potential in life in case anything happened to me during my travels. During these family meetings, we started with a devotional. Then we would sing a praise or worship song, then each of us would take turns leading the prayer. Afterward, we worked on school subjects. We rotated weekly who was in charge. The person in charge would present the devotional based on their study of God's Word. It was a blessing to be able to teach my kids how to study His

The Blooming Level (Maturing Stage)

Word. Sometimes my dear sister-in-law would come and sit in to see how our family meetings were coming along. This also helped the kids to see it as being something especially important to them.

Since I was selling many paintings and prints, I earned enough to pay my kids weekly to help me do different projects, and I taught them to manage their income and treat their chores like a job. Every month or every two months, they could decide on something they wanted to buy. They could always ask us for extra work during the week to receive extra money, and it was counted as overtime on a job. I taught them to pay 10 percent into church on Sundays, and they could give an additional offering if they felt led to. With this job system in place, another thing we discussed in the meetings was our projects in process and expectations, and we assigned action items for the week. We then did our praise reports. We also acknowledged the good things God was doing in our lives.

Eventually, I bought my son a computer because he typed the minutes up for the family group meetings. Marquice would also put them into the weekly binders that we kept. I bought my daughter, Farrah, a cash register, and she became our treasurer and reported to us about our finances. We paid monthly dues to our treasury to see how much we could accumulate to decide who and what organization or people we wanted to be a blessing to. We were doing great; the kids were doing great; and they were learning how to speak and deliver messages to a crowd, how to write and create the paperwork needed for our family meetings, how to enter the information into the computer about our bills, and how to manage their finances. And, most importantly, they learn how to put God first in everything.

Proverbs 22:6 (NKJ) says, "Train up a child in the way they should go and when they get old, they won't depart from it."

Shirley and I decided to take our kids out on camping trips and to special dinner engagements to teach them how to maintain a cordial attitude, with or without guests. They would often meet me at highlighting events, and we were always invited out to dinner by the gallery owners. Shirley and I had become immensely proud of our awesome kids and their progress.

Then Cometh Pride

But when it seems like everything is going fine, the devil will always try to show up in our lives. I was doing fantastic, the kids and Shirley seemed to be doing well, and things were flourishing. I thought that I was living on top of the world, and so self-pride began to creep into my life and my thinking. I focused on how great it felt to be a master highlighter and travel abroad to Europe, Scotland, France, Ireland, and all over the country. Since I was selling a lot of paintings while traveling abroad and doing well at my computer chip job, I was making good money. Once again, I began to get misplaced priorities and started hanging out with my wealthy friends and entertaining them. Although I was taking care of my family financially, emotionally, I was not there to meet their needs. Then 2008 came, and the bottom dropped on the entire economy in California, especially in the real estate market. I learned an especially important principle during that time of my life.

Proverbs 16:18 (NKJ) says, "Pride goes before destruction, And a haughty spirit before a fall."

I learned that I had become too confident and a little arrogant about my abilities and my present position. I realized that I was not as good as I thought. I had to humble myself and remember that it was God who had lifted me up; I had not done it myself.

Remember no matter how much our God blesses you, always remember to pray and ask Him to help you stay humble and never forget where you came from. Staying humble through times when things were going great was exceedingly difficult for me to do.

Courage through Adversity and Hardships

Well, the economy had become unfortunately bad in California's Bay Area, and the housing market was drastically dropping. So buying

The Blooming Level (Maturing Stage)

artwork was no longer a priority at the time, causing many galleries to close. Then, I was laid off from my computer chip manufacturing job and had to permanently relocate back to Madera, California. I now know that the Lord was transitioning my life again to help prepare me to discover the purpose He had planned for my life.

I joined a family community church in Fresno, California, led by Pastor Chester McGensy and his wife Janetta McGensy. I also joined their men's fellowship and accountability group.

Now, I was much stronger than before because God had brought me through many trials and deep valleys. I had persevered and overcame many difficulties in my life, so I was better equipped to handle this next trial. I was used to bringing a lot of income home from my master highlighting events, selling paintings, and my computer chip manufacturing job. All this income had suddenly stopped coming in. All the income that I had coming in now was from my unemployment check.

This created a lot of pressure again on my household. I would share with the brothers in my men's accountability group fellowship that things were getting a little tight in my household, and it was beginning to cause some friction at home between my wife and me. We prayed for the Lord to help me to find a job locally. One of the brothers in the men's fellowship invited me to a group meeting with him to a Celebrate Recovery meeting at a church in Fresno, because the program and support of the group had helped him get through a similar situation.

Later I was told about another Celebrate Recovery Group meeting held in Madera at the Valley West Christian Center. I kept attending the group meetings, and I began to work the steps of the program to really learn to deal with my character defects and insecurities. While I had combatted the alcohol and drug issues, I was still often in denial about my inability to control my anger and get upset. I also had many fears and insecurities that I had to admit to and deal with. On top of that, I still was afraid to give God total control of all areas of my life. There were a few areas that I felt that I kept stashed away in my back pockets.

My unemployment checks lasted for a while but were running out. Shirley and I would pray daily together and ask for God's help. God was faithful again and did bless me with a job at Georgia Pacific Color Box division in Madera. I was so grateful.

After working there for a while, I started a Bible study group at lunchtime with some friends, Matt, Junior, and Tino. I continued to attend my Celebrate Recovery meetings and work my steps. I believe God wanted to help me finally deal with and break some of the character defects hindering me from developing a more intimate relationship with Him. He wanted to use my life to help others conquer some of the same issues that I was dealing with and had experienced in my life. At this point, I had completely reached my bottom and realized I had some mental strongholds that were hindering me from allowing God to help me make real changes in my life. While I seemed strong in the Lord and successful, I had recently only been that way when things were going right. The moment things started going wrong, I fell apart too. So I had to go to any lengths to allow God's Holy Spirit and others in the study groups to help transform my life, so I could be strong even amid my trials like I had been in my early days.

My mom was still there for me through it all. She said, "My dear son, God loves us so much, and He has His own ways of slowing us down and bringing us back to Him. The good news is that you are much stronger, wiser, smarter, and you still have Him on your side. I want you to know that I am extremely proud of you. Mama doesn't think, but Mama knows that you are going to be all right because I can see the tremendous growth that God has developed in your life, and He is continuing to develop in you. Always remember what I taught you as a little kid: you can do and be anybody you want to be in life if you keep putting God first in your life, keep striving forward, giving Him a hundred percent, and all that you got."

I began to develop a very intimate personal relationship with the Holy Spirit in my life. I began to talk to Him daily as a friend through praying and fellowshipping with Him. I spent some time every day to allow Him to communicate back to me through His precious Word. This planned time spent with Him allowed me to get to know Him on a more personable level. Our response to our trials or situations often exposes what we really believe. I thought I really believed but found out I still had work to do, so I could remain faithful during my trials.

The Lord led me to attend a Madera Men of Integrity Men's retreat that also helped to revolutionize my life. I was amazed to see God's tremendous transformation power to heal and change so many men's lives, especially the young people. There were over two hundred men who attended the Madera Men of Integrity retreat at Camp Sugar Pine. I started to pray for and minister to many men while there. One of my dear friends, named Rod, said, "Brother Farraday, I have noticed how it seems like you have a gift to minister to and encourage other men and inspire them to grow in God. I want you to be prepared for and thinking about doing a breakout session for next year." God blessed me to prepare a message for the next year called "A Touch of the Master's Hand as We Are Rooted in Christ." The response was great, and I was told that many people were blessed who attended it.

Little did I know that the Lord was preparing me for some of the most devastating and traumatic experiences headed my way. I have learned in my life and my walk with God that at different times, I have had different levels of trust in Him. I noticed that I often could trust Him on one level, but when the situation seemed to be over my head and out of my control, I often found it exceedingly difficult to trust Him on that greater level. Sometimes we allow our fears and doubts to creep in and tarnish our view at that moment about what God can do and who He really is.

Yet, Hebrews 13:8 (NKJ) tells us that Jesus Christ is the same yesterday, today, and forever. He never changes.

The Golden Journey

Well, my next big assignment was in the making.

One morning I was talking to my mom on the phone after praying together. She told me she had been working in her garden, watering and nurturing her beautiful plants and flowers, when she slipped and fell on her left arm. I asked a friend to take her to the hospital.

Mom was brought to the emergency room to take some X-rays of her arm. Luckily, she hadn't broken any bones. But since she was an elderly woman, they asked her questions to test her memory, like who was the president of the United States and the Mayor of Galveston, Texas. Mom could not answer their questions, so they decided to send her to a skilled nursing center to get her rehabilitated.

Mom told the people that she had a little puppy at home that she needed to attend to. Because they wouldn't let her go home, Mom was upset, so they felt she was getting hostile and belligerent, and they gave her medication to sedate her.

I tried to call and get some real answers as to the drugs and medication that she was being given and why was she even sent there in the first place. But I was not given any satisfying answers.

Every time I would try to talk to Mom, she seemed to be incoherent from medication. I asked my cousin Corliss and my dear sweet Aunt Eva to check on her since I was in California.

My cousin and aunt visited Mom and checked on her puppy and the house. Corliss said Mom sat up and talked to them for a while, and she seemed to be fine until they started giving her the medication. Then moments later, she became drowsy and was unable to speak. Then thirty minutes later, when the nurses came to take her to her therapy, she could not even stand.

Finally, I got some answers. I talked to her nurse and got a list of the medications that she was being given, and I found out that they had been giving her four antipsychotic medications and four different antidepressant medications that could cause her all kinds of severe problems.

I immediately insisted they stop giving her those medications. They said, "Well, you or somebody will have to come here and attend to her because all she wants to do is go home and tend to her puppy." The nurse said that Mom becomes very defiant and tries to scratch them when she cannot have her way. So they insisted on sedating her for her protection.

Since I could not handle things on the phone, I was forced to ask God to help me go to my Queen of a Mom and get her into a stable safe place. This situation created a sense of insecurity, fear, anger, unforgiveness, and all kinds of emotional turmoil for me. I did not know what to do.

So, here I was on my last leg on my job because I had received various machine safety violations throughout my years of working there (we were only allowed two during our duration of working there), and now I was in this devastating situation with my mom. I felt insecure, but God was my refuge.

Psalm 46:1 (NKJ) reminded me that "God is our refuge and strength, A very present help in our time of trouble." So you need to keep running to God because your security can be found in Him.

I remember what my mom told me to do when I get into a desperate place like this. She told me to always pray to God and ask for his help He always answered a desperate cry. So that night, I got on my knees, and I asked the Lord to please help me to figure out what to do in this situation and to give me the wisdom I needed to make the right decisions.

During hard times, you need to learn to stand flat-footed and immovable on God's precious Word. Remember that your feelings will often affect your emotions negatively, which can cause you to start thinking the wrong way.

Proverbs 3:5, 6 (NKJ) says, "Trust in the Lord with all of your heart And lean not on your own understanding; In all of your ways acknowledge Him, And He shall direct your paths."

1st Corinthians 15:58 (in the Amplified Bible) says, "Therefore, my beloved brothers and sisters be steadfast, immovable, always excelling in the work of the Lord, always doing your best and doing more than is needed, being continually aware that your labor even to the point of exhaustion in the Lord is not futile nor wasted, it is never without purpose."

This situation brought up a lot of fear in me. I was afraid of not knowing what the outcome was going to be for my mom. I was afraid because this whole experience was way over my head and out of my control. I had no idea how the Family Medical Leave Act program worked as far as pay or time off was concerned. So, I prayed and asked for God's help.

I also felt responsible and angry for getting my mother into this situation because I suggested she go to the hospital to get her arm checked out. I was angry and unforgiving.

James 1:19, 20 (NKJ) reminded me to be swift to hear, slow to speak, and slow to anger because it does not produce the righteousness of God.

Proverbs 14:29 (NLT) says people with understanding control their anger, but a hot temper shows great foolishness.

It was clear I had to let go of my anger and deal with my unforgiveness. In my case, I was upset about the hospital staff sending Mom to the skilled nursing center without talking to me first, and I was also upset about the method they had decided to use to deal with my mom. These feelings of anger were trying to create a sense of resentment and bitterness in me.

Matthew 6:14 (NKJ) tells us the proper way to respond to unforgiveness. It says, "If you forgive other people when they sin against you, your Heavenly Father will also forgive you."

Just praying to God is a big part of you responding right to these emotions.

So, we must learn to forgive others just as the Lord commands us to maintain our favor with God, so our prayers will not be hindered. Here is a good thing to remember: no matter what situation you face, try to keep the Lord as your focus and not your problem. I have

The Blooming Level (Maturing Stage)

learned that whatever you focus on will get bigger in your mind. I've heard a pastor say, "Where the mind goes, the person follows."

Well, I can see that the Lord was faithfully continuing to walk with me through it all.

After prayer, I was led to try to make plans to go to Galveston to rescue my dear mom. I had no idea how I would get to her from Hobby Airport to Galveston, which was over fifty miles away. I did not have the money for a limousine, an Uber ride, or a taxi. But I was willing to hitchhike if necessary. After praying to the Lord, He brought a very dear friend to my mind, SanAntone. He was one of my high school friends whom my mom had also nurtured during our upbringing. I felt led to call him and tell him that I was coming to town to check on Mom. He agreed to pick me up and said I could also use one of his cars, which he was kind enough to fill up with gas, while I was in town. My little brother, James Kirk Williams, was also extremely helpful during my visit to Galveston. God was so faithful during this ordeal.

I could see the Lord was faithfully continuing to walk with me through it all. Once I arrived at the nursing home, my dear mom saw me, and we kissed and hugged each other for a long time. We talked and prayed together. She told all the nurses and staff members that my precious son from California had flown in to check on his mama. I stayed all night in Mom's room to make sure all her medication had been stopped. I wanted to evaluate her condition for myself. The next morning when we got up, I observed their care routine, and I assisted them with every part of it. Without any medication, Mom was beginning to be mom again. I said, "Thank you, Jesus. Now, will you please guide me and show me what to do next?"

After talking and praying with my cousin Corliss, we arranged a meeting with mom's care staff. Now with the entire staff on board, it was so much easier for us to establish a plan to help bring my mom back up to speed with her therapy and to help prepare her to qualify for Medicaid to go into the chosen nursing home.

My dear brother Clarence Jr. came and stayed a day with Mom, while Corliss and I went to check out different care facilities. My dear cousin and I prayed together, and we asked God to show us the right one to choose. After discussing each of them, God gave her and me the same answer.

I still had one more crucial decision to make concerning my mom's house in Texas. God blessed me to talk to a lady at the new permanent nursing home who was familiar with these types of Medicaid situations. She sent me to one of her attorney friends, who instructed me on what to do. I had to get the house cleaned out and ready to rent for me to keep it. Corliss and I were still praying. She was continuously walking with me daily through every situation.

It had taken me three weeks to progress this far with Mom's situation. And now, my biggest problem was I only had one more week left from my FMLA time off to get rid of over fifty years of things accumulated throughout the years of her living in the house.

I cried during every decision that I had to make, especially when it came time to give or throw away many of her things. We didn't have the money to put them in storage. I also had to sell a lot of the furniture and other items to help pay the attorney's fees to file the necessary paperwork for me to keep the house. With tears in my eyes, I made every decision to do what I had to do.

Well, after being at the facility for a month, Mom was trying to get adjusted to her new place. Corliss would go and visit her often to assist with her staying groomed. She found Mom a beautician in the area and would go and pick her up every two weeks to get her hair done. Mom's precious granddaughter Latoya would go to visit her regularly and give her a manicure and pedicure.

My dear Queen of a Mom had a great upbeat personality, and she would use her walker to go and assist the other patients in the facility. Unfortunately, she had a habit of smoking, but this was a no-smoking facility. A couple of friends of mine would go to visit her and see how she was adjusting and doing in her new home. One day Mom asked one of them for a cigarette since she saw the package

The Blooming Level (Maturing Stage)

in his front shirt pocket. Since he didn't know the rules, he gave one to her. Mom later went to the restroom with some air freshener and smoked that cigarette.

The next day I got a call from the administrator telling me what happened. I said, "I'm sorry I don't know how she got it, but I will talk to Mom about it." I discussed the problem with her, and she agreed not to do it again. She did mention to me that she had noticed other people smoking outside in another area.

Well, the time was passing, and I was thinking about trying to set up another visit to Mom. I was concerned about having any more vacation time left because I thought I used it all during my FMLA leave. I prayed to the Lord and asked Him to help me to go and see Mom again.

One day, I was invited to lunch by a dear friend and brother in Christ named Chuck Hayward. He said, "Brother Farraday, you and your dear mom have been weighing heavily on my mind. Can we meet for lunch at Carl's Jr. and pick up a burger and chat for a minute?" I said sure.

So, Chuck and I met for lunch. We prayed for the food and asked God for His spiritual insight to view my situation through His eyes.

We also asked Him to please give us the wisdom and knowledge to know what to do in this case. Chuck said, "It sounds like nobody is going to be able to satisfy your mom and take good care of her like you. I believe you should pray first and seriously think about bringing your mom here to California to stay with you."

The enemy tried to bring up some of my concerns and insecurities in my mind. California nursing homes were expensive, and I had to start all over with her medical process in California because they were different from Texas created a big concern for me. I wasn't sure I would be able to care for her in California, and my vision was blurred because of my financial, spiritual, and physical concerns at the time. I was exhausted from thinking too much,

My brother Chuck said to me, "It is your mom, my dear brother, and remember we only get one of them." I thought about what my

Queen of a Mom would do if the shoe was on the other foot. I knew that she would, without a doubt, bring me with her and trust the outcome to God.

At times in your life, God will be working behind the scenes on your behalf to orchestrate and arrange your situations to meet His Divine Purposes in your life.

The Bible says, in Isaiah 55:8, 9 (NKJ), "For My thoughts are not your thoughts, nor are your ways My ways, says the Lord. As the heavens are higher than the earth, so are My ways higher than your ways and My thoughts than your thoughts."

A few days later, a close friend of the family called me from Texas. He said, "Brother Farraday, the Lord put it on my mind to give you enough money to come down and visit your dear mom before Christmas to help you both adjust to the new environment that she is in." I told him I had already used all of my vacation time left during my FMLA leave.

Timing is everything with God, and His timing in this matter was perfect. While I was at work one morning, I asked my supervisor where he had me working that day, and he said, "Farraday, I have you scheduled off for this week on vacation unless you want to save it to use later." I said, with tears of joy streaming down my cheeks, can I use my vacation time later to go and see my mom in Texas? He said, "Sure, just give me the dates, and I will try to help arrange the time off for you." I had forgotten they had required us all to choose one week we wanted for our vacation time, and then we had a raffle for who got the first pick.

I hurried up and called my dear friend back and told him what God miraculously had done. I still had a week of vacation time that I could use. God was so faithful and good.

There is no situation that is too hard for our God to handle. Therefore, no matter what obstacles the enemy may try to throw in your way to stop you from reaching your full potential in God, he cannot succeed. Therefore, I want you to know without a doubt that our God Can Do The Impossible.

Matthew 19:26 (NKJ) says, "But Jesus looked at them and said to them, With men this is impossible, but with God all things are possible."

Days later, Mom had made many good friends with the other elderly people in the facility. She was very thoughtful and helpful to them. The patients who lived there were financially secure. One month, Mom was even chosen as the queen of the facility.

One day a few of the patients noticed that Mom looked sad and asked her what was wrong. She said, "They will not give me a cigarette where I can go outside in the smoking area to smoke." The patients had their relatives and grandkids go and buy mom over ten cartons of cigarettes.

A few days later, I received a call from the administrator again, and she said, "Farraday, as much as we love your dear mom, she has got to go because someone has given her over ten cartons of cigarettes. This type of behavior will have all our patients defiant. I need you to help us move your mom to another facility, and besides, she will not listen to anybody but you." I believe this was God giving me confirmation about what brother Chuck and I had discussed about bringing my mom back to California.

The Golden Walk

I now had a scheduled trip to go and get my mom to return to California with me. Rosalind, my dear cousin, had agreed to pay for my mom's and my flight back to California. My cousin Corliss and her husband, Pastor Harry Allen, agreed to pick me up at the airport and provide me with a rental car during my visit. This time God had provided everything.

When I arrived at the nursing home, my mom smiled while waiting patiently to go with me on another exciting adventure. Mom and I hugged each other tightly and prayed together. We gazed at each other, and Mom said, "Well, my dear son, with God's help, we will make it through this."

I am reminded of two verses that would be good for you to remember and meditate on during times like these in your life.

Philippians 4:19 (NKJ) says, "And my God shall supply all of your needs according to His riches in glory by Christ Jesus."

Romans 12:2 says, (paraphrased) Do not copy the world's way to respond to things but be transformed by the renewing of your mind. Think about your situation the way God does are sees it. When you do that, you will realize that He is still in total control, and He will guide you and lead you through your situation victoriously.

My niece Latoya drove down from Houston to see Mom one last time, and she pampered her with a beautiful manicure and pedicure.

The next morning, I woke up early while everyone else was still asleep, and I spent some time praying and thanking God for the many provisions he had provided for my dear Queen of a Mom and me. I asked for God's continued favor and traveling mercies for a safe drive home from the airport in California.

Well, we did make it safely to San Jose's airport. We had a three-hour drive to Madera, and we sang together and listened to praise and worship music all the way home.

I still had a few days off from work when we got back, which was good as we needed the time to get Mom settled in. The Lord had led me to find a primary doctor for Mom to see in Madera upon her return. I took Mom to visit the doctor and the Social Security office.

I had the church, and my men's accountability group, praying for Mom and me to get God's favor with the Medi-Cal process. During our initial visit at the Social Services office, an administrative manager, who was leaving for the day, noticed the love and care that I was rendering to my mom. She said, "I am retiring in three weeks, but I want to schedule an appointment with you and your mom, and I will personally see that you both get taken care of and get everything you need before I retire." Mom and I prayed together again and thanked God for His miraculous favor and perfect timing with meeting that manager. Amazingly, the manager did exactly what she said, and Mom was approved for Medi-Cal with all the benefits.

After getting Mom settled in properly to this new environment with me in Madera, we developed a weekly routine. God was so faithful to us during this time. I was still working for Georgia Pacific/Color Box division, and now I was approved to be her primary provider, and they would pay me and allow me to hire others to take care of my Queen of a Mom. After several months, God sent us a jewel of a provider named Cindy Wilson. Mom and I will always be thankful for her wonderful services and care.

Once or twice a month, Mom would go with me to present my gospel message to the people at the Madera Rescue Mission. I would always allow her to give them a brief word of encouragement, and she was always thrilled to do so. She also prayed for them and blessed the food. We had become partners and soldiers for the Lord as we purchased and gave out Bibles to many people for years.

God miraculously restored all my financial issues concerning both houses, the ones in Texas and California. God also allowed me to buy my Queen of a Mom a brand-new wardrobe. I tried to help her not think about all the clothes I had to discard in Texas during this transition. I would try to joke with her by saying, "Mom, you are in California now so that you would need a change of wardrobe anyway." She would say, "Yeah, but I had some nice things to wear to church to go and serve the Lord." I said, "I know, sweetheart, but the good news is that you are here with me." She would hug me and agree I had a point, saying, "I know as long as we have God and each other, everything is going to be all right."

The Golden Crown

Dear reader, one of my most important goals is to help you increase your faith muscles along the way, learn the incredible value of developing a personal relationship with God, and learn about His faithfulness and awesome love for you. So, hopefully, that has been happening. Keep that goal in mind as we move forward.

Everything was moving forward for me, and we were making progress. It had been exceedingly difficult for me to get Mom's birth certificate because, during her upbringing in Louisiana, which was in 1931, they could freely change their names on their own if they did not like it. Therefore, it took me over three months to get my mom's birth certificate, and we found out that her original name was something else.

For Christmas, I wanted to take my mom on a cruise or a trip out of state. After dealing with a lot of red tape, I secured her a passport. Since I was qualified to be her primary care provider, they were paying me to do this.

Two weeks before we departed, Mom said, "I believe we need to go to the doctor to check out the left side of my chest because, at times, it has been hard for me to breathe, and occasionally, I have chest pains on that side that bothers me." So I took her to the emergency room. They ran all types of tests and performed numerous X-rays on her chest cavity.

I was so excited about our upcoming Christmas trip that I had the entire team in the emergency room all excited about our upcoming cruise. The doctor said, "I do see a spot on the left side of her lung cavity, but it could be pneumonia. So, I will give you guys some antibiotics before your trip to help with the pneumonia problem. I want you to take her on the cruise, and I will prescribe you both some tablets to take to avoid getting seasick during your trip. And, don't worry, they have doctors on the cruise ships if you experience any problems. So go and have a great time!"

Mom and I went on the cruise and had an exciting and enjoyable time, filled with lots of food and entertainment on the cruise. We went to comedy shows, acrobatic shows, and a variety of plays. The ambiance of the different dining restaurants was so great and memorable, and the food was delicious.

I also took her on a fantastic excursion to Ensenada, where we were amazed at the beauty of the city. We enjoyed our precious time together, laughing, hugging, shopping, praying together, and thanking God for these precious moments.

The Blooming Level (Maturing Stage)

Once we returned home, we made an appointment to go to her primary care doctor. She looked at the X-rays and sent us to a cancer doctor.

Then came her diagnosis. After doing a biopsy, we were told that she had a form of cancer. We prayed together before taking any additional full-body test to determine if it had spread to any other area of her body. The results were good; no other areas were found. Mom and I prayed and cried together, thanking God that it was not as bad as it could have been. After embracing my mom with a great big hug, I asked her what she wanted to do.

She amazingly said with exuberance and determination, "Son, Mama loves you from the bottom of my heart, and I want you to always remember that. All Mama wants to do is to spend as much time that I can with you, enjoying this wonderful life that the good Lord has given us both. I want you to always remember what I taught you when you were a little kid, and that is to keep putting God first in your life. Keep striving forward and giving Him a hundred percent and all that you got, and then you can be and do whatever you desire in your life. Now let us both wipe these tears from our eyes and go and have some fun together thanking God for every moment of it!"

God gave us His grace by giving my dear Queen of a Mom and me an entire year of enjoying our time together.

During that time, we developed a routine. We would pray together each morning, I would prepare her a delicious morning breakfast, and I would feed her puppy, who was so protective of her. Then Cindy would tend to her while I was at work. I also took Mom biweekly to a wonderful faith-filled beautician named LaVena Edwards, to keep her hair looking great, and they shared many great conversations.

We both got monthly manicures and pedicures at The Queen Bees Nails and Spa, and we took memorable photos together during the process. The employees often commended me for treating my mom like a queen.

As time passed, her illness began to progress.

I took her and her dear health provider, Cindy, to Monterey, California, where we rode on a triple-seated bicycle down the

Fisherman's Wharf to Lover's point. We also took Mom to Monterey's wonderful aquarium and to eat a delicious dinner at the Old Fisherman's Grotto Restaurant.

We were given awesome window seat views, where we could see people kayaking as we ate our superb dinners. On one trip to Monterey, Mom surprisingly took a ride with me out in the water on a Kayak.

God was so good to us, and He blessed us to take her chihuahua puppy, Smokey, with us on an adventurous steam train ride at The Roaring Camp in Santa Cruz, California. We enjoyed having an exciting weekend together with her puppy on the beaches in Santa Cruz.

As Mom's condition continued to progress, I brought family members out to celebrate with my dear Queen of a Mom for one last time to create more wonderful memories. We went to places like Yosemite Valley and San Francisco, where we rode the city bus tours, and we ate in marvelous seafood restaurants on the Embarcadero.

We then headed to LA, enjoying our time with her for the last time as a family group. We all prayed together and thanked God for the wonderful memories that He allowed us to share.

As her condition began to worsen, I had to get Mom oxygen to take along with the wheelchair. The nurses said they thought that after the next two weeks, Mom would not be able to travel any longer.

I talked to my cousin Corliss and told her I wanted to do something really special for her last trip.

So, I planned a trip to take her to ride the dinner and wine train in Napa Valley. I also booked us a bed and breakfast for one of the days in Calistoga.

In honor of the occasion, I wanted to get her a crown and a nice dress. My cousin Corliss suggested that we look online to find the right crown, preferably one with her name on it, especially since her name was Elizabeth. I ordered her a custom crown with "Mom Queen Elizabeth" on it. This was on a Monday, and the company said that it may be delayed until the following Monday due to the

The Blooming Level (Maturing Stage)

engraving needed. I prayed and asked the Lord what to do because I needed the crown. I was led to go to a place downtown where they sold tuxes and dresses for special occasions, and I asked the lady for a queen's crown.

I told her that it was for my terminally ill mom, and I wanted to crown her as the queen of my life. The lady was so thrilled, and tears began to fall from her eyes. She said, "Son, that is such a great gesture to your mom. The regular price is eighty-five dollars for this crown, but I will give it to you for thirty-five. May God bless you and your dear mom." I thanked the lady and gave her a great big hug. When I got home, I tried the crown on my mom. She was so thrilled and excited about our trip.

It was an exceptionally amazing trip. We rode to Napa Valley Friday, and I went to see where the wine train was located when I made it in town to prepare my mom to be ready and on time for the next day's exciting dinner train ride.

When I went to the desk to confirm our train ride and dinner reservations for Saturday, I told the attendant that I was taking my terminally ill mom on this dinner train ride to enjoy her last days together with me. Still, I sure wanted to get her a horse and carriage ride because I had purchased some crowns, and I wanted to crown her as the queen of my life. I told her I had called several places throughout the week, but no one was still doing it at this time of the year. Tears started to fall from her eyes as she found five numbers for me to call in the Napa area to try and get this horse and carriage.

I tried to call the first three numbers, and the people said they were closed for the season. I prayed again.

When I dialed the next number, the lady said, "I am not doing it now, but I have a friend who might be able to accommodate you, but she lives an hour and a half away from where you are now, but if you can take the mountain route, you can get there in forty-five minutes." God was faithful. I booked the horse and carriage for Sunday after I left the bed and breakfast.

I came back to the desk attendant, and I gave her a great big hug, and she confirmed that we were scheduled for a wonderful train ride and delicious steak dinner with dessert as we toured Napa Valley tomorrow.

I also asked the lady about any great restaurants. She told me about a few, and I took Mom to an exceptionally fine restaurant with a jazz concert right next door with Herbie Hancock, who happened to be playing that night. Once I heard that I knew I wanted tickets, but they had recently sold out. However, when I told them my plans, they created a spot at a special table right in the front row. We had a blast, but we left early because she was tired, and I did not want to tire her out.

For those of you who still have moms, please cherish and value them because we only get one. Whether you are caring for your elderly parents or any other situation that you face that may seem impossible, I am here to tell you that your God is walking with you, and He is willing and able to do exceedingly, abundantly, above, all that we may think or ask. You must always remember that all things are possible to those who believe, trust, and obey Him.

When I got my Queen of a Mom back to our room, we prayed together and thanked God for our safe arrival and wonderful time tonight. We also asked Him to please bless the rest of our weekend.

The next morning, I got up early, and I went and found a nice breakfast place while Mom rested.

Soon it was time for the tour. We had such a marvelous dinner and touring train ride. We then headed to Calistoga, which was an hour's drive away. I took her to a restaurant there that night for a light snack because we were still full after that fantastic dinner on the train ride.

The next morning, we had a wonderful breakfast brought to us in our rooms. I told the lady who owned the bed and breakfast about Mom's condition, and she made it so incredibly special for Mom by giving her several memorable presents.

After checking out, it was time for the grand finale of all the events coming. I was now taking her to the place where I would crown her as "the queen of my life" as she experienced riding off into an imaginable sunset in a white horse and carriage that the Lord had provided for us.

Well, after driving across the many curves in the mountains for forty-five minutes, we came to this beautiful ranch. Mom fell in love with the white horse. I faced Mom in her wheelchair, got on my knees, and crowned her the queen of my life as the lady videoed it. Mom was so happy as tears rolled down her cheeks. Then the lady allowed the queen to step up in the carriage. Mom was so extremely happy and overwhelmed with excitement.

I videoed her riding around the wide, stable area of the ranch, and I said, "Wave, Mama. Wave Goodbye to the people," and as she waved, I said, "Lord, here comes your queen, now receive her in Jesus's mighty name. Amen."

Conclusion:
Your Turn to Discover the Real You in Christ

Well, my dear readers, I would like to first congratulate you on a job well done in continuing with me on this miraculous journey. That tells me that you have lots of courage, have staying power, and are dedicated to reaching your full potential in God and your life.

God began to open my spiritual eyes to see life in a whole new way. This new life of seeing and understanding is way beyond anything magical. It is an awareness and understanding of attaining a new life, right here on earth, while gaining an intimate personal relationship with God through His Holy Spirit.

That is exactly my deepest desire for you today. My sincere prayer is for God's Holy Spirit to help illuminate the eyes of your understanding. The very first thing I want you to understand, my cherished reader, is this race is not given to the swift but to those who endure to the end. This is not a quick fix or quick sprint, but rather, it is a marathon to the pathway in your life to becoming the best you can be with the help of God's Holy Spirit. So, let's get ready, get set, and now let's go running toward this fulfilling life and opportunity to discover the real you in Christ.

Salvation Is Key to Obtaining Your Helper

The first step is to make sure of your eternal destiny and to obtain your everlasting helper, who is the Holy Spirit.

Please repeat this prayer after me.

Dear, Lord Jesus, thank you for dying on the cross for my sins. Please forgive me. Now would you come into my life and save me? I receive You as my Lord and Savior.

Now please help me to live for You the rest of my life. In Jesus's mighty name, I pray. Amen.

Once this prayer is said from your heart, the Lord honors it and will give you a new life and quicken you with a real helper, the Holy Spirit. You now have a new nature and help to succeed in this spiritual journey.

Romans 8:11 (NKJ) says, "But if the Spirit of Him who raised Jesus from the dead dwells in you, He who raised Christ from the dead will also give rise to your model bodies through His Spirit who dwells in you."

New Creation in Christ

You are now a new creation in Christ.

2nd Corinthians 5:17 (NKJ) says, "Therefore if anyone is in Christ, he is a new creation; all things have passed away, behold, all things have become new."

This is also one of many promises that the Lord has given to you. This new birth experience is the beginning phase of a fresh start and the beginning of discovering the real you.

Our sins have now been forgiven and removed. Hallelujah, no more guilt and shame. The Holy Spirit comes to dwell in us and live Christ's life through us. We are born afresh; therefore, we can never go back to what we once were because we have been born into Christ's life. We have been given a new spirit and a new nature.

Ephesians 1:13 (NKJ) says, "In Him you also trusted, after you heard the word of truth, the gospel of your salvation; in whom also, having believed, you were sealed with the Holy Spirit of promise."

The Bible says the Holy Spirit lives in us from the moment that we are saved and accept Jesus Christ as our Savior, and He never leaves us.

Renewing of the Mind

Our desire should be to continue to be conformed to the image of Christ. This process is called the renewing of your mind.

Romans 12:1, 2 (NLT) says, "And so, dear brothers and sisters, I plead with you to give your bodies to God because of all that He has done for you. Let them be a living and holy life—the kind He will find acceptable. This is truly the way to worship Him. Do not copy the behavior and customs of this world, but let God transform you into a new person by changing the way you think. Then you will learn to know God's will for you, which is good, pleasing, and perfect."

You might wonder how in the world you are going to be able to do that. Alone, you absolutely cannot do it. But now you have a helper: the Holy Spirit who lives on the inside of you who will help you to do all things.

To renew your mind, follow these steps:
- Pray daily and ask the Holy Spirit to protect your mind, give you wisdom and direction.
- Spend quality time with Him reading and meditating on His Word daily while reading to get an understanding and to obtain knowledge and wisdom to apply the information to your life.
- Be sure to not only read His Word for understanding but also to actively listen through your spirit to what the Holy Spirit wants to say to you about your life.
- Be mindful of your negative thought patterns, and at the onset of them, be ready to cast them down and bring every one of them back under the protection of the Umbrella of God. This means to bring or change those thoughts to who God says you are as one of His precious kids. Remember, you are a king's kid!

- Watch what you say to yourself and others. Speak words of life to yourself and others daily. Write down or record short affirmations to listen to daily to help remind you of who you are in Christ.
- Repeat these things above daily until they become a natural part of your life.

Philippians 4:13 is a good reference scripture to look at to verify that you can do it. "I can do all things through Christ who strengthens me."

Father God, I pray that You would supernaturally help whoever is reading this book right now in Jesus's mighty name.

I pray that the eyes of their understanding would be enlightened to know exactly what the hope of Your calling is in their lives in Jesus's mighty name.

I pray that You would help them to practice this information above to assist them to renew their minds and to learn how to speak life daily to themselves and others.

I pray that they would be sustained and strengthened with Your might and power to start on the pathway of discovering the real them in Christ. Amen.

The Value of God's Word

The precious Word of God is the mind of God on paper. So, you need to live His Word.

The Holy Spirit will assist you in applying God's Word in your life. Then you will begin to learn how to cooperate and submit yourself to Him.

We must learn how God views us as one of His precious children. We must learn to obey Him. God works through His ways and not ours.

I want you to know right now that there is real power in the Word of God when you believe and apply it in your daily life.

Psalm 139:14 (NKJ) says, "I will praise You, for I am fearfully and wonderfully made. Marvelous are Your works, And that my soul knows very well."

Hebrews 4:12 (NKJ) says, "For the Word of God is living and powerful and sharper than any two-edged sword piercing even to the division of Soul and Spirit and of joints, and marrow, and is a discerner of the thoughts and intents of the heart."

God's Word is alive; it is more than just mere words on paper. When believed by faith and applied to your life, it can manifest great results. When you are feeding on God's precious Word, it is like filling yourself with God's dynamite to defeat the spirit of darkness.

We Must Learn to Walk By Faith

Are you hoping and desiring for some things to happen in your life? Things like becoming the person God is calling you to be and reaching your full potential in God? Faith is necessary and important to God.

In the book of Hebrews 11:1 (NKJ), it says, "Now faith is the substance of things hoped for, the evidence of things not seen."

Faith is being confident that the Lord will do exactly as He promises you. We must believe that God can and will do what He says He will do. He is faithful. But we must also remember this scripture in Hebrews 11:6 (NKJ), which says," But without faith it is impossible to please Him, for he who comes to God must believe that He is, and that He is a rewarder of those who diligently seek Him."

You can increase your faith in many ways:
- Read and meditate on God's precious Word daily.
- Strive to learn who you are in Christ as one of His kids, meaning get to know your benefits, His promises to you and that He loves you unconditionally.
- Remember your past victories He has brought you through.
- Share your testimonies with others.
- Pray regularly for God to increase your faith muscles in Him.
- Get to know the Holy Spirit intimately by reading about Him in the Gospel of John chapters 14, 15, and 16. These chapters tell you all about Him and His purposes in your life.
- Memorize foundational scriptures in areas that you struggle with. To do this, find an area of difficulty that you are

struggling within your life and ask the Holy Spirit to illuminate the scripture that will give you direction and solutions to know how to apply it to your life.
- Keep a journal and write down your prayer request and praise reports from God's answered prayers. Review them frequently. Remembering that God does not change.
- Associate yourself with positive faith-filled people to increase your faith and then be a bright light and witness to others about what God has done for you in your life.
- Watch what you think and say daily, and try to speak life to yourself and others.
- Put your faith in action day after day and stand flat-footed on God's Word and promises.

We Are in a Spiritual War

I want you to know that you are in a spiritual war. As you work on building your faith, Satan will work on tearing it down.

I can recall when I first came to know I was a child of God, and I would get into a misunderstanding with one of my friends. I used to think he was my enemy; therefore, I would retaliate by saying and doing hurtful things to get back at him. Once I began to gain some spiritual knowledge and insight about my new identity in Christ and the devil was tempting and confusing me, I began to see and respond differently to things. The Holy Spirit opened my spiritual eyes to many things. I began to pray for those who despitefully misused me, like God's Word told me to do. I began to not focus so much on his actions, but I thought about what I could do to improve our friendship. I learned to be humbler by listening to see if there was an underlying problem that I could assist with God's help. I learned that a soft answer would turn away strife, but grievous words could stir it back up.

My dear reader, I want you to know that you are not fighting against your mate, kids, parents, friends, coworkers, or any other people with whom you may be having difficulties with. No, you are fighting the devil. He desires to steal, kill, and destroy you and your precious family, and he does that by helping your character defects flourish. Therefore, you must allow God's Holy Spirit to guide you for you to come out victorious.

Ephesians 6:11 (NIV) says, "Put on the full armor of God so you can take your stand against the devil's schemes."

Ephesians 6:12 (NIV) says, "For our struggle is not against flesh and blood, but against the rulers, against the authorities, against the spiritual forces of evil in the heavenly realms."

Keep Feeding Your Spiritual Baby

I want to share this analogy with you to try to help make this illustration live in your thinking and your life. You know I have two precious kids, and when they were first born, one of the things I learned is when I held them, I needed to place my hand behind their neck because the neck had not been fully developed yet. We fed the babies formula initially and then some food when they were old enough.

After about six months, when I would pick them up, an amazing thing happened. They could hold their heads up on their own. Enough time had passed, and enough food had been given to the babies to develop and strengthen their necks.

This leads me to ask you a question, "How much spiritual food are you feeding your spiritual baby on the inside of you?"

I often minister to and hear other people say, "Brother Farraday, I have been praying a lot, but I continue to struggle with and repeat some of the same bad behaviors in my life." The same way your natural baby needs food, you must learn to feed your spiritual baby too. You must feed your spiritual baby enough spiritual food to give him the courage, desire, and strength to help you to yield to your helper on the inside of you, who is the Holy Spirit. He will give you the knowledge, wisdom, and power to resist temptation and defeat the enemy of your soul.

The spiritual food that you need to feed your spiritual baby is:
- The precious Word of God
- Prayer
- Praise and Worship

And you need this food daily. In daily feeding the baby inside you, you are learning how God thinks of you as one of His precious children. You are learning your position and the benefits of being a King's kid. God promises us numerous blessings as children of the Highest God.

When we feed our spiritual baby with prayer, we communicate our deepest desires and concerns to God. Prayer really does strengthen your spiritual baby and your confidence in your Savior and Redeemer. Remember that prayer changes things.

You should also feed your spiritual baby through praise and worship. When you are feeding on praise, you are thanking God for the many blessings that He has given to you. When you feed your spiritual baby through worship, you are worshipping God for who He is. The precious Word of God tells us that He will come and live in your praise and worship.

Therefore, remember to keep feeding your spiritual baby the food it needs daily to strengthen you and enable you to reach your full potential in God as you discover the real you in Christ.

I Will Fear No Evil

I realize that at times this journey of discovery is not always easy to walk in. But I want you to know and be confident that you are more than a conqueror in Christ (Romans 8:37).

He will strengthen you daily as you learn how to cooperate with your newly realized spiritual helper, the Holy Spirit who resides in you.

I am reminded of a great scripture found in Psalms 23:4 (NKJ) that I want you to remember and meditate on often. This verse says, "Yea though I walk through the valley of the shadow of death, I will fear no evil; for You are with me; Your rod and Your staff, they comfort me."

Psalms 23:1 (NKJ) says, "The Lord is my shepherd; I shall not want."

This beautiful Psalm is a reminder to us that the Lord is a caring God. Like sheep, we all have gone astray, but our God will still bring us back into His fold and give us the provisions and care we need. But we need to believe in Him and ask Him to guide us.

In the book of Philippians, the Lord promises us He will supply all of our needs according to His great riches in glory by Christ Jesus.

We can have confidence that while we are encountering our darkest valley experiences, our God, who is our Divine Shepherd and has His rod of power in one hand and His Blessed Grace in the other, will give you whatever you need to live a victorious life as you discover the real you in Christ.

I Will Never Forsake You or Leave You

In closing, my dear and valued reader, I want you to be assured of this one thing, the Lord your God will go with you whether it is in your most joyous moments or in your most difficult times. He is committed to you, and He will always work for you because He has your best interest in His mind.

In Deuteronomy 31:6 (NKJ), Moses is speaking to his people, and today, I can hear, through my spiritual ears, that same message from God's precious Word speaking to you: "Be strong and of good courage, do not fear nor be afraid of them; for the Lord your God, He is the one who goes with you. He will never leave you nor forsake you."

Always remember that no matter what obstacles may try to hinder you from reaching your full potential in God, your God has already prepared a secure pathway for you to get through it. Therefore, if you continue to keep your eyes on Jesus and do not fear, He will certainly lead you in the best possible way to discover the real you in Christ.

Father God, Mr. Holy Spirit, and our precious Lord Jesus, I lift every reader of this book to You.

I pray that You will draw them into a closer and more intimate relationship with You, once they are saved and get to know their real helper, who is the Holy Spirit inside of them.

I pray that the eyes of their hearts would be enlightened right now to know the hope to which they have been called.

Now I commit every reader into the care of Your mighty hands, and I thank you on credit for helping to strengthen them in their inner being to become the person you have called them to be.

Amen.

Let's Connect

- Don't forget to grab your free Interlude: "Your Turn Releasing Past Hurts, Negative Habits, and Hang-Ups," at www.farradaywilliamsauthor.com.
- Stay informed about my next inspiring and encouraging books coming soon through farradaywilliamsauthor.com.
- Connecting with you is important to me! Do you need prayer? Please e-mail your prayer request at farradaywilliamsauthor@gmail.com
- Invite me to speak about "Discover The Real You" by contacting me at farradaywilliamsauthor@gmail.com.

How Can You Help?

If *Discover the Real You: Release Past Hurts, Negative Habits, and Hang-Ups* blessed you,

please leave an Amazon review. It will help others to discover their real self.

★★★★★

Your review matters!

About the author

Farraday Williams, a native of Galveston, Texas, has had the privilege of speaking for The Madera Rescue Mission, Celebrate Recovery groups and men's accountability groups. Since overcoming past hurts, negative habits, and hang-ups, and forming an intimate relationship with his Savior, he desires to help others come to Christ and reach their full potential, learning, as he did, to walk with faith.

At one point in his life's journey, he was blessed to be a master highlighter for Thomas Kinkade, which allowed him to use his artistic talent and spiritual gifts to bless others. During those ten years as an "ambassador of light," he uplifted, encouraged, prayed for, ministered to, and inspired many people.

He chose to write this book, sharing his life experiences so that others could reach their full potential in God, and he could reach a wider audience.

When he isn't volunteering for various church functions, speaking for church organizations, or working, he can be found writing, painting, and enjoying his family and grandkids. He hopes to leave behind a legacy of helping people choose to believe, trust, and obey God.

Website: farradaywilliamsauthor.com

Email: farradaywilliamsauthor@gmail.com

www.ingramcontent.com/pod-product-compliance
Lightning Source LLC
Chambersburg PA
CBHW071457070526
44578CB00001B/377